John Cage and Buddhist Ecopoetics

NEW DIRECTIONS IN RELIGION AND LITERATURE

This series aims to showcase new work at the forefront of religion and literature through short studies written by leading and rising scholars in the field. Books will pursue a variety of theoretical approaches as they engage with writing from different religious and literary traditions. Collectively, the series will offer a timely critical intervention to the interdisciplinary crossover between religion and literature, speaking to wider contemporary interests and mapping out new directions for the field in the early twenty-first century.

ALSO AVAILABLE FROM BLOOMSBURY:

Blake. Wordsworth. Religion, Jonathan Roberts
Do the Gods Wear Capes?, Ben Saunders
England's Secular Scripture, Jo Carruthers
Glyph and the Gramophone, Luke Ferretter
The Late Walter Benjamin, John Schad
The New Atheist Novel, Arthur Bradley and Andrew Tate
Victorian Parables, Susan E. Colón

FORTHCOMING:

Faithful Reading, Mark Knight and Emma Mason
Rewriting the Old Testament in Anglo-Saxon Verse, Samantha Zacher

John Cage and Buddhist Ecopoetics

PETER JAEGER

New Directions in Religion and Literature

BLOOMSBURY
LONDON · NEW DELHI · NEW YORK · SYDNEY

Bloomsbury Academic

An imprint of Bloomsbury Publishing Plc

50 Bedford Square   1385 Broadway
London   New York
WC1B 3DP   NY 10018
UK   USA

www.bloomsbury.com

First published 2013

© Peter Jaeger, 2013

All rights reserved. No part of this publication may be reproduced or transmitted in any form or by any means, electronic or mechanical, including photocopying, recording or any information storage or retrieval system, without prior permission in writing from the publishers.

Peter Jaeger has asserted his right under the Copyright, Designs and Patents Act, 1988, to be identified as Author of this work.

No responsibility for loss caused to any individual or organization acting on or refraining from action as a result of the material in this publication can be accepted by Bloomsbury Academic or the author.

British Library Cataloguing-in-Publication Data
A catalogue record for this book is available from the British Library.

ISBN: HB: 978-1-4411-0466-3
PB: 978-1-4411-1752-6
ePDF: 978-1-6235-6234-2
ePub: 978-1-6235-6543-5

Library of Congress Cataloging-in-Publication Data
A catalog record for this title is available from the Library of Congress.

Typeset by Deanta Global Publishing Services, Chennai, India

In the land of perfect freedom there are no words
(The Lankavātāra Sutra)

Contents

Acknowledgements viii

Introduction 1
THE IMITATION OF NATURE IN HER MANNER OF OPERATION 7
NOT JUST SELF- BUT SOCIAL REALIZATION 115

Endnotes 167
Works cited 173
Index 183

Acknowledgements

My gratitude goes to the Arts and Humanities Research Council for funding research expeditions and time away from university duties during the completion of this book. Thanks also goes to Laura Kuhn at the John Cage Trust, Bard College, N.Y. and to the Getty Institute in Los Angeles, for permission to access archival material. Tim Atkins, derek beaulieu, Nancy Gillespie, Harry Gilonis, John Havelda, Jeff Hilson, Jenna Kotch and Ruth Windle deserve thanks for providing research leads and for helping to clarify my thought on Cage and on some of the text's theoretical background. Thanks also to Charles Bernstein, Marjorie Perloff, Robert Hampson and Frank Davey for their continuing interest in my research. John Gaynor, Doug Landles, Michael Barbour, Zoketsu Norman Fisher and Bhadra warrant special thanks for their advice and example pertaining to the *Dharma*. This series' editors Mark Knight and Emma Mason have been wonderfully supportive through the various stages of this book's production. Their advice has been invaluable.

John Cage and Buddhist Ecopoetics has grown out of several talks and short articles which have appeared in earlier forms and contexts. Thanks to Jerzy Kutnik for arranging to have a short section translated into Polish by the "Crossroads" Centre for Intercultural Creative Initiatives and published in *Cage 100* (2013), and to Emmanuelle Waeckerle for publishing an excerpt in the Yorkshire Artspace and University of the Creative Arts co-publication *Booklive!* (2013). I would also like to thank the organizers and support staff of the many conferences and public lectures where I have presented parts of this book during the John Cage centennial year: David Ayers, organizer of the *Material Meanings* Conference hosted by the European Network for Avant-Garde and Modernism Studies, University of Kent, Canterbury, England; Desmond Biddulph and Louise Marchant of the *Art History and Culture Talks* series at the Buddhist Society, London; Nik Cesare and Matt Jones, organizers of the *Future of Cage: Credo 100* conference, University of Toronto, Canada; Jerome Fletcher at

Performance Writing 12, the Arnolfini Gallery, Bristol, England; Nancy Gillespie at the Kootenay School of Writing in Vancouver, Canada; Robert Hampson at the Contemporary Innovative Poetry Research Seminar, Royal Holloway College, University of London; Kevin Killian for hosting a talk and reading based on this research at the California College of Art in San Francisco; Jerzy Kutnik at the *John Cage 100 Symposium* held in Lublin, Poland; John Lo Breglio and Eoin Flannery at the English and Modern Languages/Europe-Japan Research Centre, Oxford Brookes University, Oxford; Michelle Naka Pierce of the *Jack Kerouac School of Disembodied Poetics* for inviting me to participate in the *fourthirtythree: Caged!* event at Naropa University in Boulder, Colorado; William Rowe and Stephen Mooney at the *Poetry and Revolution International Conference*, held at the Contemporary Poetics Research Centre, Birkbeck College, University of London; Nicola Sim at the Whitechapel Gallery in London for organizing a talk on Cage; Emmanuelle Waeckerle, organizer of the *Book Live Symposium* at the London South Bank University.

Thanks also to the various publishers who have agreed to grant permission to quote from their books. Quotations by John Cage from *Silence*; *A Year From Monday: New Lectures and Writings*; *M: Writings '67–'72*; *Empty Words: Writing '73–'78*; *X: Writings '79–'82*; *Anarchy* (Wesleyan University Press) © 1961; 1968; 1973; 1978; 1987; 1988, reprinted by permission of Wesleyan University Press. Quotations by John Cage from "Overpopulation and Art" in *John Cage Composed in America* (University of Chicago Press) © 1994, reprinted by permission of the University of Chicago Press. Quotations from John Cage's personal correspondence held in the David Tudor Papers at the Getty Insitute in Los Angeles, with permission of the John Cage Trust. Quotations by Allen Ginsberg from *Collected Poems 1947–1997* (HarperCollins) © 2006, reprinted by permission of HarperCollins Publisher. Quotations from *Peace is Every Step: The Path of Mindfulness in Everyday Life* by Thich Nhat Hanh, copyright © by Thich Nhat Hanh. Used by permission of Bantam Books, a division of Random House, Inc'. Quotations by Leslie Scalapino from *How Phenomena Appear to Unfold* (Potes and Poets, 1st edition) © 1989 and from *New Time* (Wesleyan University Press) © 1999, reprinted with permission of the Estate of Leslie Scalapino. Quotations by Gary Snyder from *The Gary Snyder Reader: Prose, Poetry, and Translations*

(Counterpoint Press) © 1999, reprinted by permission of Counterpoint. Quotations by Philip Whalen from *Collected Poems of Philip Whalen* (Wesleyan University Press) © 2007, reprinted with permission of the Estate of Philip Whalen.

A special note of thanks to my family, who put up with my near-constant absence while thinking about nothing. This book is for you.

Introduction

In 2012 the celebrated pianist and interpreter of John Cage, Margaret Leng Tan, contributed a talk and performance to the Cage centennial celebrations in Lublin, Poland. Tan's talk focused primarily on Cage's interest in Zen, paying special attention to his understanding of time and space as it pertains to his Buddhist faith. She spoke of Cage's Zen-influenced belief that time and space are inseparable and that in fact Cage thought these two categories were *alive*; for Tan (and Cage) the living relationship between space and time is what distinguishes Asian thought from the philosophies of the West. Tan also pointed out that much of Cage's work embodies the concurrent unfolding of time and space. After the talk, Tan circulated a photo-copied sheet of paper containing short excerpts drawn from news media reports about ivory poaching. The paper was also stamped by hand in green ink with the phrase: 'TOY PIANOS DON'T KILL ELEPHANTS' an allusion to the various pieces that Cage wrote specifically for the toy piano during the 1940s. She then performed the infamous *4'33"* of 1952 on a toy piano, as well as Cage's 1959 piece *Water Walk*. Tan's talk and performance brought together the important relationship between Zen and ecological awareness that informed Cage's work, not only in his role as a composer of music but also as a visual artist and writer. Although these three fields of Cage's cultural production were highly inter-related, it is this last area of his activity – his writing and poetics – that this book seeks to address. How did Cage's understanding of Zen and his concern for environmental issues impact his writing? To what extent did the interface of these two concerns spill over into other issues raised by his 'lecture-poems' and poetry, such as his turn towards indeterminacy and chance operations in the 1950s and his later work's support for non-violent anarchism? And what do his challenge to more conventional modes of making meaning, his frequent use of blank space as a visual poetic element, and his embrace of the illegible, have to do with his Zen Buddhist ecopoetics?

This book situates Cage's Zen poetics in the context of debates about contemporary ecocriticism. Jonathan Skinner has pointed out that this emerging critical discourse has tended to privilege the referential function of language, in which poets refer 'outside' of the poem to a 'natural topos' (128). This approach – when taken by both poets and critics – cannot help but reference literary convention and the pastoral tradition. A good example of this sort of contemporary ecocriticism can be found in J. Scott Bryson's anthology of essays *Ecocriticism: A Critical Introduction* (2002). Although Bryson cautions that any definition of the term ecopoetry should remain fluid, he considers ecopoetry as a 'subset of nature poetry that, while adhering to certain conventions of romanticism, also advances beyond that tradition and takes on distinctly contemporary problems and issues' (5). Ecopoetics, for Bryson, supports a belief in the interdependence of the world, a humble appreciation of wildness, and a 'scepticism towards hyperrationality and its resultant overreliance on technology' (7). Yet the critical focus of Bryson's anthology – with its high stress on ecological content – tends to elide formally innovative writing, in favour of paraphrasing the ecological themes found in examples of historical and contemporary 'nature' poetry. *John Cage and Buddhist Ecopoetics* presents an alternative approach by considering Cage's formal innovations as integral to his ecopoetics. The book takes as a starting point the argument that Cage's nature writing is not limited to representing the thematics of nature, or to reiterating references to natural scenes existing 'outside' of the poem's language. Cage as ecopoet is not merely concerned with representing natural phenomenon, but also with exploring the materiality of linguistic phenomena *as nature*. In Skinner's account, ecopoetics investigates the social, economic and linguistic framing of nature, while simultaneously exploring how each of these frames might undergo a process of disintegration. And it is precisely this disintegration, this Cagean *'nothing to say'* or Zen-inflected space of illegibility for the representation of nature, that this book attends to.

Cage's introduction to Zen Buddhism and his developing awareness of the religion are clearly elucidated in recent texts such as Kenneth Silverman's *Begin Again* (2011) and Kay Larson's *Where the Heart*

Beats (2012). This book shifts perspective from these and other similar accounts of Cage in two key ways. First, the book focuses specifically on the 'green' or ecological dimension of Cage's Zen poetics, and then relates that topic to his later work's concern for social liberation through anarchist politics. Secondly, and perhaps more significantly, this book takes a cue from Cage and from other work on innovative poetics, in order to explore the notion that critical writing can become 'the subject of its own engagement, giving itself over to the dangers and fluidities and challenges of that possibility' (Spahr 7–8). Cage's writing offers exemplary possibilities for the production of an engaged, performative literary criticism, because his own critical and exegetical work frequently paved the way by employing such unorthodox approaches as the use of collage, disjunction, chance operations and/or unconventional page layout. I am using the term *performative* in the sense given to it by Mieke Bal in *Travelling Concepts in the Humanities* (2002). For Bal, the performative 'lives by the present and knows no alterity' (17). I focus specifically on Bal's definition of the performative due to its immediacy, its temporal presence and its claim for non-dualistic awareness – categories of experience which can also be found represented in the literature of Zen. One aspect of Bal's discussion of performativity is the concept of the theatrical *mise-en-scène*, which she redefines provisionally as 'the materialization of a text – word and score – in a form accessible for public, collective reception' (97). *Mise-en-scène* is performative in Bal's terms to the extent that it provides a space or environment in which something takes place on a social scale, in a 'limited and delimited section of real time and space' (97). Cage's work similarly performs its Zen content at a formal, material level, and functions as a textual *mise-en-scène* for the emptiness of the Buddhist void.

Cage was an innovator in many fields, and his exploration of new, performative ways to write expository prose (in texts such as the lecture-poems found in *Silence*) parallels his similar explorations with collage and chance operations in music, visual art and poetry. Crucial to his writing practice was the discovery of chance operations, a compositional procedure which allowed him to reduce personal intention. In a 1982 interview with Cole Gagne and Tracy Caras, Cage mentions that his first inclination after encountering Zen was to make music about Buddhist ideas, but then he thought, 'instead of talking about it, to do it; instead of discussing it, to act it out. And that would be done by making the music non-intentional' (71–72). Cage began using chance operations in 1951, when he was given a pocket version of the *I Ching* by his student, the composer Christian Wolff. This ancient Taoist book of oracles accords with the Buddhist principle that the universe is impermanent, existing as it does in a continual state of flux. Cage used the text to determine such compositional factors as the number and duration of sounds in a musical composition, or the choice and placement of words in writing.

Originally, Cage threw coins in the traditional manner prescribed by the *I Ching* to determine the formal features of a composition. During the late 1960s, however, he made his first experiments with computer-generated compositional methods based on the *I Ching*, and in the early 1980s he began using IC (*I Ching*), a computer programme developed by his assistant Andrew Culver to speed up the generating process. This approach 'revolutionized' Cage's working practices, because all he had to do was refer on the computer printout to the hexagram, use that hexagram as numerical data for determining compositional form, and then to cross out the data and move on to the next hexagram (Nicholls 99). It is important to note that Cage was 'less interested in the *I Ching* as a book of wisdom than as a mechanism of chance operations that produces random numbers from 1 to 64' (Lewallen 235). The point of relying so heavily on the oracle was not to receive arcane solutions or esoteric knowledge, but to compose intricate scores based on numerical values, and to reconfigure subjective intention by limiting choice. Following Cage's use of digital *I Ching* software, I employed an online random-integer generator to organize this book's layout. I first programmed the online generator to produce a random sequence of numbers running from one to sixty-four (the number of possible combinations or hexagrams used in the oracle). Next I divided the text into short units by counting out the exact number of words for each unit – the number of words per unit being derived from the number generated by the random series. I then programmed another series of numbers between one and six (*I Ching* coins are thrown six times in all, giving a hexagram of six lines). These numbers determined the number of spaces between each unit of text. Hence, the number of words per unit of text, as well as the number of spaces between each unit, has been determined by chance operations, limited by the structure of the *I Ching*'s numerological constraints. The resulting text is subject to odd interruptions, offbeat *lacunae* of silence, each of which has been dictated by a non-subjective agency. It is my hope that the rationale for this unconventional approach will become fully evident to readers as they negotiate their way through the book. The text's blank spaces and quirky, uncomfortable line endings are intended to reinforce, at a formal level, numerous Cagean concerns, including not only his interest in the Buddhist void but also his explorations of textual materiality, the operation of nature and boredom.

The book is divided into two sections. The first part, entitled 'The Imitation of Nature in Her Manner of Operation,' after a phrase frequently employed by Cage, considers his understanding of Zen Buddhism in relation to his ecopoetics. It focuses primarily on the lecture-poems collected in *Silence*, as well as on his texts *Empty Words* and *Mureau*. Crucial to my discussion is Cage's materialist exploration of silence and poetic language as means to signify the Buddhist void. The second section centres on Cage's engagement with the social and with his support for anarchist politics. Entitled 'Not Just Self- but Social Realization,' this part reads Cage across the grain by reconsidering his writing and politics in the light of thinkers and writers not normally associated with his work. Primarily, this section employs psychoanalytic theory, a discourse which Cage set himself at odds with, but which nevertheless might still provide us with a useful means to reconsider some of the psychological and social features of his cultural production. My return to the more politicized aspects of Lacan and to post-Lacanian theory is not intended to limit our experience of Cage, but to see how psychoanalysis might allow us to ask certain questions about Cage, about his understanding of Buddhism, about his politics and about his representation of nature – all of which might otherwise remain unquestioned. In any event, the tension formed between discursive text and silence in *John Cage and Buddhist Ecopoetics* is fully intended to provide readers with a performative site for Cagean indeterminacy, and for the Zen-inspired 'nothing' which resides at the heart of his work. In words borrowed from Cage's contemporary, the French philosopher Gaston Bachelard, '[h]ow should one perform the image of nothing if not by exaggerating it?' (219).

When Andrew Schelling asked the poet and Zen monk Philip Whalen if he thought his poetry provided a form of Buddhist Dharma teaching, Whalen replied in the affirmative, and wondered if it was possible for someone who was already practicing Zen to 'get the point' while other people who weren't practicing might say, 'What is this practice thing about, what is Zen about?' (232). Crucial to the spread of Buddhism in North America and Europe was the way in which the religion was disseminated through poetic texts, in forms that were significantly challenging to the established literary context. Whalen, Kerouac, Ginsberg and the Beats were central to this dissemination at the populist level, but no less so than Cage, whose influence on such practices as sampling, digital writing, performance art and aleatory writing will arguably prove more long lasting than the influence of the Beats. In any case, neither Cage nor the Beats composed work in the form of the traditional lyric or confessional poem, with its insistence on the self-present subject who typically ruminates on a serious topic and who often arrives at a pithy conclusion or psychological insight through metaphor or other type of figurative language. Why this congruence of literary experimentation and the emergence of Western Buddhism? Charles Bernstein has argued that stylistic innovation in poetry is recognizable not only as an alternative to aesthetic convention, but also as an alternative type of social formation (227). If Buddhism contributed to the critique of Western social organization that occurred during the 1950s and intensified during the 1960s, it did so through the deployment of aesthetic forms which similarly intervened in the traditional, socially-accepted norms of cultural production. Cage's Buddhist Ecopoetics played a key role in this cultural intervention.

THE IMITATION OF NATURE IN HER MANNER OF OPERATION

'These "lectures" – in which discontinuity in the form of silences no longer than punctuational pauses and abrupt shifts in subject matter, tempo of delivery, and other aspects have been brought about mainly by chance operations and materials for realizing musical compositions indeterminate as to performance – are really Cage's first published poems'

(Mac Low 215)

It may be enlightening to begin by comparing Cage's use of blank space in his 1959 text 'Lecture on Nothing' to Charles Olson's discussion of the temporal qualities of open field notation.[1] In the influential essay 'Projective Verse' (1950), Olson describes how the graphic organization of space on the page represents time: the larger the space, the longer the silence between words. Olson writes: '[i]f a contemporary poet leaves a space as

long as the phrase before

it, he means that space to be held, by the breath, an equal length of time' (245). By aligning spatial form

with time, Olson provides a means to chart a physical body in writing, to present text as a temporal indicator of

breath and of lived experience. Similarly, Cage's

'Lecture on Nothing' is printed in columns 'to provide a rhythmic reading, and his "Composition as Process"' (1958) segregates sentences into short

lines, in which 'each line of

the text whether speech or

silence [requires] one second for its performance' (*Silence* 18). The similarity in graphic notation between Cage and Olson is not to imply that the two writers shared the same overall poetic agenda.

Where Olson wanted to chart the moment by moment movement of perception ('one perception must immediately and directly lead to a further perception' [240]), Cage was more interested in emancipating the writer from subjective intentions altogether. And while Olson criticized what he called the 'lyrical interference of the individual as ego' (59) due to his interest in areas as diverse as quantum mechanics, topology, phenomenology, mythology and linguistics, Cage's critique of the ego during the 1940s and 1950s was rooted more closely in his interest in Zen. He describes his compositional method as a 'reflection' of his 'engagement in Zen' (*Silence* ix), and questions the Dada impulse in the light of Zen by pointing out that 'Dada nowadays has in it a space, an emptiness, that it formerly lacked. What nowadays, America mid-twentieth century, is Zen?' (xi). Indeed, what is the space of Zen – that is, what is the material site of this space, and how can it be represented? Cage here uses the word 'Zen' to indicate a new phase of the Dada impulse, which he transplants from its European roots into an American context marked by space and emptiness. Much like Olson's spatial notation, the blank spaces and durational stops and starts in Cage's texts generate a series of temporal pauses which serve as sites for embodying a physical, material experience of

time. ¶ 'What I do,' writes Cage in the 1961 foreword to *Silence*, 'I do not wish to blame Zen, though without my engagement with Zen [. . . .] I doubt whether I would have done what I have done' (xi). Why Zen and silence? Instead of considering silence

as the expressive or emphatic time lapse between sounds (or words), silence for Cage is variable and impermanent. The world 'teems' with sounds, he writes, and 'is in fact, at/no point free of/them' (*Silence* 23). Sound for Cage is all pervasive, and in his work the notion of silence becomes a

sign for something other than the absence of sound. Two Buddhist stories come to mind:

in the *Mumonkan*,

a thirteenth-century collection of *kōans*[2] compiled by the Chinese Zen master Wumen (Japanese: *Mumon*), a

philosopher asks the Buddha, 'Without words, without the wordless, will you tell me the truth?' The Buddha keeps silence until the philosopher bows and thanks him, saying: 'With your loving kindness,

I have cleared away all my delusions and entered the true path.' When the Buddha's senior disciple Ananda asks his teacher what the philosopher had attained, the Buddha replies:

'A good horse runs even at

the shadow of the whip' (Reps 116).³ The second story is drawn from the *Vimalakrīī Nirdeśa*, an early Mahāyāna scripture which is also foundational for Zen. The Buddha sends numerous Bodhisattvas to discuss the falseness of dualistic views with Vimalakīrti. After expounding their position, the Crown Prince Bodhisattva Mañjuśrī asks Vimalakīrti to expound his own view. In response, Vimalakīrti keeps silent, and Mañjuśrī applauds his

silence: 'Excellent, noble sir! This is indeed the entrance into the non-duality of the Bodhisattvas. Here there is no use for syllables, sounds, and ideas' (Thurman 77). Just as silence in these early Buddhist texts is not the 'mere absence of speech or words,

but a means to eloquently communicate' (Chandrakanthan 145), Cage's use of the term 'silence' indicates something other than the

conceptual idea of silence. ¶ Cage revised his 1955 lecture 'Experimental Music' for inclusion in *Silence* by adding a dialogue between an uncompromising teacher and unenlightened student, and by appending the word 'doctrine' to the lecture's title. The introduction to this lecture

states that both revisions refer to *The Huang-Po Doctrine of Universal Mind* (13), a text which had recently been translated by John Blofeld and published by the London Buddhist Society. In an interview

with Daniel Charles, Cage placed this ninth century *Chàn* Buddhist text on his

list of most important books (*For* 227). For most Buddhists, 'doctrine' normally means a systematic presentation of teachings, usually taken from the scriptures and roughly equivalent to the terms 'Buddhist thought' or 'Buddhist philosophy' (Sangharakshita *Essence* 23). True, Cage's lecture does follow the form of the Huang-Po text by presenting some of Cage's key ideas about the creative process in the form of

a dialogue. But in what way could Cage's lecture on experimental music be considered a doctrine? Here is where Zen specifically differentiates

itself from forms of Buddhism which rely more on the logically coherent exposition of the Dharma, in favour of a direct transmission of the living spirit of Buddhism. A good example of this form of transmission can be found in the story of Mahākāśyapa, one of the Buddha's oldest and most austere disciples. Most likely Cage would have been

familiar with

this story through his attendance at Suzuki's lectures or through its inclusion in Suzuki's *Essays in Zen Buddhism* (1949). In any case, Zen Buddhists regard the story of Mahākāśyapa

as a formational moment in the history of their school. When a large crowd of Bodhisattvas, celestial beings and human followers of the Buddha gathered to hear him teach, he refrained from speaking and simply held up a golden flower. Mahākāśyapa understood the meaning of the Buddha's gesture and

reacted to it by smiling. The Buddha responded to this smile by addressing the entire assembly: 'I have

the most precious treasure, spiritual and transcendental, which this moment I hand over to you, O venerable Mahākāśyapa!' (Suzuki *Essays* 167). In other words, the Buddha transmitted the essence of his teaching to his disciple, without recourse to linguistic exposition; his speech about entrusting the Dharma was purely for the benefit of the

other sentient beings gathered around him. This story would certainly have informed the early *Chàn* masters, who considered Mahākaśhyapa to be the first patriarch of their faith, and who traced the continual

lineage of Dharma transmissions through twenty-eight Indian and six Chinese masters. From this perspective, Cage's silence echoes what Huang-Po calls the 'Highest Vehicle' of Buddhism, which 'cannot be communicated in

Words' (13). Moreover, Cage's silence further reiterates the Huang-Po doctrine's description of the void as 'omnipresent, *silent*, pure' (emphasis added; 22), and its description of the realization of enlightenment as the attainment of *nothing*: 'the Buddha said: "I attained

nothing from complete, unexcelled

enlightenment"' (25). ¶ Along

with the Huang-Po doctrine, Cage often refers to texts on Zen by Suzuki and by Alan Watts, and he was a keen reader of L.C. Beckett's 1955 book *Neti Neti*, a text which borrows from twentieth-century physics and from

Hindu, Zen Buddhist and Christian Mystical traditions, in order to address the questions of how to make the 'thinker silent' (88) and how

to bring 'action from out of *silence*' (emphasis added; 68). Suzuki touches on this form of non-thinking silence when he portrays emptiness, or *śūnyatā*, as one of the most important and

puzzling notions of Mahāyāna Buddhism (*Manual* 29), and describes

it in his commentary on *The Zen Doctrine of No Mind* (1949) as a pure 'nothingness [. . .] the negation of all qualities,

a state of absolute no-ness' (27). In *The Way of Zen* (1957), Watts writes that the awareness of *śūnyatā* entails a demolishing of all conscious and unconscious premises of thought and action, until 'the very depths of the mind are reduced to a total silence' (83).[4] Silence, nothing, void: Cage's employment of these terms, drawn as they are from

historical and contemporary Zen literature, is consistent with the Mahāyāna Buddhist claim that phenomena have no substantial

identity or independent being. It is not that things do

not exist, but that they are empty or 'void' of independent existence, and the aim of Buddhist practice is to break down the delusion that phenomena (including the self) exist apart from their dependency on other phenomena.

In the context of Cage's studies of Zen Buddhism, having 'nothing to say' but 'saying it' would appear to suggest an attempt to signify the emptiness of *śūnyatā*; Cage presents us with a self that communicates in language, although what

it communicates is entirely void. ¶ The paradox of 'saying nothing' is reminiscent of the use of language as a 'skill in means' (*upāya*) employed by Buddhist

teachers to help their students attain insight. Jackson Mac

Low comments that Cage thought of his chance operations and indeterminate compositions as skilful means to help sentient beings attain enlightenment and suggests that Cage viewed the 'experiences of composing, performing and hearing such works as being equally conducive to the arousal of *prajña* -intuitive wisdom/energy, the

essence/seed of the enlightened state' (211). As the 'educational and ethical equivalence of emptiness,' the concept of 'skill in means' is a form of teaching 'delivered relative

to context' (Williams *Buddhist* 170). In other words, the Buddhist teacher skilfully uses any appropriate means to lead students towards an awareness of emptiness, including not only the teacher's ethical behaviour and compassion, but

also their use of language. The fourth-century CE *Yogācarā* school of Buddhism, for example, explicitly teaches that, while on the one hand language can be 'used to structure reality, culturally, in terms of ego

and object,' language can also be used to 'reveal reality at a level beyond the ego/object schema' (Miller 44). Zen also uses language in the form of paradoxical poems, anecdotes and *kōans* to help free its adherents' attachment to delusion. Cage's 'saying nothing' does not establish meaning, although it reveals through language and silence

the tradition of Buddhism in a contemporary Western setting. Poetry functions here as an appropriate 'skill in means,' an innovative form of Dharma teaching delivered to a particular social and aesthetic context. ¶ In 1958, Cage delivered a lecture in Brussels entitled 'Indeterminacy: New Aspects of Form

in Instrumental and Electronic Music.' This lecture, which was followed by a piano recital by Cage and David Tutor, consists of thirty-three very short stories, which Cage delivered at a rate of one per minute. If the story was extremely short, Cage would have to draw it out, but if it was relatively long, he would have

to speak rapidly in order to deliver it within the one minute time constraint. Cage writes that he put the stories together in an unplanned way, in order to suggest that 'all things – stories, incidental sounds from the environment, and, by extension, beings – are related' (*Silence* 260). Marjorie Perloff describes how in *Silence,* the expository discourse of the lectures give

way, at unexpected junctures, to the short narratives of Cage's versions of Zen *kōans* (*Poetics* 309). For example, 'One Sunday morning, Mother said to Dad, 'Let's go to church.' Dad said, 'O.K.' When they drove up in front, Dad showed no sign of getting out of the car. Mother said,

'Aren't you coming in?' Dad said, 'No, I'll wait for you here' (*Silence* 85). As Perloff suggests, Cage's stories do bring to mind the pithy anecdotes and *kōans* of the Zen tradition, which Zen teachers use as skilful means to lead their students towards enlightenment. Zen stories make no pretence to logic and often focus on seemingly trivial, unimportant details and events. Case 7 of the *Mumonkan*, for instance, relates the story of a monk who has just entered a monastery, and who asks the master Jōshū for instruction. Jōshū responds by asking him if he has eaten his rice gruel yet, and when the monk answers by saying that he has already eaten, Jōshū instructs him to wash his bowls. At these simple words, the monk attains some realization (Yamada 40). Cage's stories similarly tend to focus on seemingly trivial details. They also frequently side-step common-sense resolution. In one short narrative, for example, Cage writes about the pianist David Tudor and a student at Black Mountain College. The student questions Tudor while he eats his lunch, but Tudor ignores the student's question. The student persists, until Tudor finally looks at him and says, 'If you don't know, why do you ask?' (*Silence* 266). The

Dialogue – if you can call it that – is typically obscure. There is a question, but we do not know what it is, and the teacher's response is completely

opaque. Compare this story with

the illogic of a well-known Zen *kōan*: 'Master Bashō said to the assembly, "if you have a shujō [staff], I will give it to you. If you have no shujō, I will take it away

from you"' (Yamada 208). Much like Master Bashō's contradictory statement about giving something to someone who already has it, and taking something away from someone who does not have it, Tudor's answer foils any logically determinate answer. In Zen terms, we could say

that Tudor's answer echoes Master Bashō's attempt to confuse the intellect, to move his student into a non-conceptual experience

of emptiness, towards the realization of *śūnyatā*. ¶ Cage's *kōan*-like short stories,

with their stress on absurdity, paradox and indeterminacy, bring to mind a joke which the French psychoanalyst Jacques Lacan was fond of telling his students and colleagues. In the 1964 version of the joke, one character tells another he is catching a train for

Lemberg: 'Why are you telling me you are going to Lemberg'? The other replies,

'since you really are going there, and that, if you are telling me this, it is so that I shall think you are going to Cracow?'(*Four* 139). In the 1957

version, however, Lemberg is labelled Cracow,

while Cracow is labelled Luov (*Écrits* 173). This shifting of city names emphasizes the first point of this short narrative: meaning lies not in a single signified but in the relation between signifiers and the social agreement which gives those signifiers meaning. Secondly, while only one of the characters knows his real destination, his attempt to communicate through language fails. The joke thus reveals

how truth and error are linguistic constructs which have no bearing on the Lacanian Real, that unspeakable register which is entirely beyond the capacity of language to represent. When Cage's story represents Tudor's

response to his student's question ('If you don't know, why do you ask?') as a kind of terminal punch line to a joke, he similarly short-circuits the relationship between truth and falsehood. There is in this story no logical answer

and nothing to say. In fact, Tudor's non-answer does not communicate information in conventional terms at all. It does, however, communicate a desire

for an experience that is beyond the capacity of language to address or conceptualize. This underlying desire is precisely what makes Cage's stories resemble the traditional *kōan* literature. ¶ Perloff argues that Cage's versions of the *kōan* put more stress on irrationality and absurdity than they do on the attainment of *satori* (309). While it is true that Cage's interest in Dada[5]

provides a precedent for the absurdity of his stories, his heavy preoccupation with Zen suggests that the stories offer at least an attempt to signal this crucial Buddhist goal. *Satori* is the

Japanese term given to the moment of ultimate realization or enlightenment in Zen, and as such it indicates the most vital experience for the Zen practitioner. Suzuki claims that it is essential to have

a *satori* experience in order to understand Zen (*Living* 45), and he further links *satori* to the term *kenshō*, which he defines as 'seeing into one's own nature' and 'putting an end to all forms of dualis' (69). Of course, this own nature mentioned by Suzuki does

not indicate one's unique and individual essence, a concept which Buddhists would consider

to be a delusion perpetuated by the unenlightened self in its desire to grasp something substantial and enduring. Cage's short stories function like *kōans* in as much as they frustrate the rational mind's attempt for semantic resolution.[6]

¶ Along with anecdotes written by Cage, *Silence* includes several short aphorisms drawn directly from the Zen tradition: 'Before studying Zen, men are men and mountains are mountains. While studying Zen, things become confused. After studying Zen, men are men and mountains are

mountains' (*Silence* 88). Cage's inclusion of this story in *Silence* illustrates the core Mahāyāna vision of emptiness as an ineffable and unconditioned nothing which does not exist as a substantial entity, but which is immanent, appearing as it does in the conditioned world of forms. Buddhists refer to this immanent aspect of the void as *tathatā*, meaning thusness or suchness, and the sutras sometimes refer to the Buddha Śākyamuni as the *Tathāgata*, meaning 'he who is thus gone.' Suzuki comments that suchness is the condition of things as they are in themselves: 'such as they are, no more, no less' (*Living* 73). Men

and mountains are empty to the extent that they have no enduring, individual essence, *and* they appear in the world of form, just as they are, made of earth, stone, water and so on, each of which is equally empty. Here Zen awareness cancels the distinction

between form and emptiness. Not only do *Silence* and other texts by Cage attend to formal structure and technical discipline in order to provide 'a means / of experiencing / nothing' (114); his texts also stress the importance of making an 'identification with what is here and /

now' (46) and on seeing and hearing 'each thing directly as it is' (276). Cage thus presents readers with one of the central doctrines of the Mahāyāna middle way, a path which reflects on the essential emptiness of

all things, and which transcends all dualities and all conceptual logic. As the contemporary Buddhist scholar Sangharakshita puts it, followers of this path seek to achieve a state of consciousness in which things 'exist in a state of

"unimpeded mutual solution," each interpenetrating all, and all interpenetrating each' (*Crossing* 67). ¶ Cage's indeterminate stories do not appear only in his lecture on Indeterminacy. The entire text of *Silence* is peppered with short stories, some written by Cage, some drawn from Meister Eckhart, Sri Ramakrishna or the literature surrounding

Zen, and some related to him by friends. Cage suggests that his stories could be read in the manner that one reads newspapers – that is, by 'jumping here and there and responding at the same time to environmental events and sounds'

(261). By organizing his text in such a way that it

offers readers the opportunity to dispense with linear narrative in favour of a disjunctive 'jumping' between passages, Cage creates a performative and indeterminate composition – a form of imprecise and unspecified compositional structure which Bryan

Simms has labelled as 'indeterminacy of performance' (357). This form of indeterminacy stems from Cage's innovations in musical composition; during the early 1950s, Cage departed from traditional music notation in favour of composing music with graphic scores, where space on the page might represent time or the frequency of sonic events. His unorthodox approach to notation

indicates a distinct difference between composition and performance. Because the graphic score does not include a regular time signature or other conventional means to notate sound, the performer 'cannot determine exactly what effect the notation causes – thus, indeterminacy' (*For* 135). Spatial notation is also evident in his writing practice – not only in relatively early examples such as 'Composition as

Process' (a text which

graphs each line for a one-second performance duration), but also in his later work, such as the Zen-inflected *Empty Words* of 1975:

```
            [. . .] e pr           t rth
     a         cci
     s                          nth tnt         w ea ndD
  r    strh                il   o   rv                 lm
       dn                  l                c nly w  'scoh
                        f a o p    th
     vwh tht ha ght

     r h.    H o i sh
```

THE IMITATION OF NATURE IN HER MANNER OF OPERATION 27

                       oe
         rg o   v. Gwnth dth
tak [. . .] (68).

Without a conventional time-signature or performance direction to indicate the exact duration of silences and sounds, this composition leaves space for the reader/performer to linger on silence, before moving

on to the next semantically indeterminate group of phonemes. Indeterminacy of meaning is thus yoked together with indeterminacy of performance. ¶ How do these inter-related forms of indeterminacy impact on Cage's

Zen aesthetic? Mieke Bal's discussion of Giovanni

Bernini's seventeenth-century sculpture *The Ecstasy of St. Theresa* provides a lucid example of the performative in the realm of religious representation, and her work may shed some

light on Cage's performative writing of the Zen void. The standard account of this sculpture considers it as an ekphrastic translation of the saint's ecstasy into

stone, and for this reason the sculpture serves as a demonstration of mysticism's challenge to language. Bal points out that in this view, mystical experience 'comes after the shattering of language, and is situated in a void, which requires a new mode of "speaking"

as such' (78). Bernini's sculpture

is performative in the sense that it is a form of acting, a theatrical event staged in marble, which has repercussions for the social reception of mysticism; the relevance of the sculpture

for the social 'lies in its extension of the *semiotics* of mysticism into the wider range of human experiences that it encompasses, that is, into a semiotics of the

failure of meaning production' (79). Cage's writing follows suit: first, his spatialized nothing performs the impossibility of representing Zen awareness in language; one could say that the nothing of Cage acts out a new mode of non-speaking, which is necessary for the translation of Zen experience into text. His nothing bypasses the communicative conventions of 'ordinary' language altogether. Secondly, Cage's nothing extends the semiotics of the void towards the social, towards readers who learn about and experience the void through non-semantic and performative indeterminacy. In Cage, language acts within the *mise-en-scène* of Buddhist emptiness. Here,

language stages itself as the territory of a failed semiotics, where signification provides a negation of meaning. And significantly for the social, this failure of language performs the role of

śūnyatā in the culturally-shared theatre of reading.

¶ Indeterminacy of meaning and performance brings to mind the Buddhist concept of *anupalabdhatva*, or incomprehensibility, a term which refers to the ultimate nature of things as incomprehensible and ungraspable to the ordinary mind (Thurman 161).[7] The illogic of Cage's anecdotes and his performative textual gesture ensures that ordinary, conditioned thought patterns become inoperative,

because indeterminacy calls into question the subject's illusory

sense of certainty

about phenomena or about the self. In Buddhist terms, the conditioned, subjective mind is unable to comprehend its own inability to comprehend, although it is able to cultivate a sense of *tolerance* (*kṣānti*) towards the incomprehensible. How does this tolerance operate? If I am uncertain about a concept or an experience, or if I become

aware of a certain ambiguity in my own consciousness, I do not try to control that ambiguity by clasping on to a fleeting and fictitious sense of conviction or assurance, but try instead to observe that uncertainty with a sense

of open-minded acceptance. There is no grasping involved in the practise of

kṣānti; as

Cage repeatedly reminds us, indeterminacy entails giving up personal intention and diminishing authorial control in favour of acknowledging a wider, less containable condition of experience. ¶ The

non-dualistic, non-hierarchical quality of Buddhist philosophy provides the rationale behind the Japanese Zen saying '*nichi nichi kore ko niche*,' meaning 'every day is a good

day' (or 'every day is a beautiful day') – a phrase which Helen Luckett reports was also a favourite saying of Cage (62), and which Cage uses to begin the 'Communication' section of his 'Composition as Process' lecture (*Silence* 41). The phrase comes from *Kōan* 6 of the *Biyàn Lú* (Japanese: *Hekiganroku*), or *Blue*

Cliff Record, an eleventh-century collection compiled by the Zen master and poet Hseueh-tou (*Setchō*). In this *kōan*, master Yúnmén (*Unmon*) addresses an assembly of monks, saying that he is not asking them about the days before the fifteenth of the month, but about the

days after the fifteenth. 'Come and give me a word about those days,' he remarks, and when the monks are stumped, he

himself gives them the answer: 'Every day is a good day' (161). Katsuki Sekida's commentary on this text points to the Zen stress on living with awareness of the present moment. Unlike adults, Sekida explains, children live in a constant state of positive awareness, and hence 'everything is alright, and every day is a good day' (Sekida 162).

Zen awareness is similar, in as much as neither the Zen adept nor the child make a conceptual separation between

one day and the next. They live, as the phrase

goes, in the proverbial now – a non-dualistic experience of time which comes about with the elimination of self-centred thinking. The Zen adept's response is one of thankfulness towards the myriad things, all of which are empty of

spatial and temporal characteristics. Cage's 'Composition as Process' similarly shows an acceptance of, and

gratitude towards, phenomenon. The text elides the dualistic distinction between self and other, because it consists of quotations drawn from a number of sources, including Cage's own writing (41). His re-written composition is thus 'authored'

by others, in a move that calls into question the re-writer's 'authority' as progenitor of the work. The writing becomes effortless, a gift from another which is gratefully accepted through the text's process of composition. In fact, the phrase 'I have nothing to say and I am saying it' makes another appearance among the intertexts of 'Communication' (51) thereby further illustrating

that Cage's 'I' is dispersed, empty of individual substance, and not limited to a single,

autonomous location. How can a reader know which bits of writing originate with Cage, and which bits originate elsewhere, sourced as they are from an array of other writings, other territories, other subjects? Perhaps from a Zen perspective, every text is a good

text. ¶ When Cage states: 'I have nothing to say and I am saying it and that is poetry as I need it,' his use of the first-person pronoun is not to be taken as the misrecognition of self as a coherent ego, an 'I' who is able to speak and to make decisions freely and apart from other phenomena,

and who is able to answer with the name 'John' or with the word 'I' to the question 'who is speaking?' There is, of course, a self who is evident here, who

speaks nothing, and who needs poetry,

but in the context of Cage's engagement with Buddhist *śūnyatā* this self appears to be equally void, equally empty of essential identity. Instead, Cage's 'I' must be considered as a 'no-self' (*anātman*), a self that stands opposed to belief in a permanent, unified

and self-contained identity. As Moncayo writes, for Buddhism, 'true self is no-self because phenomena in their own being are empty and only exist as a function of their relationship with everything else [. . .] emptiness in Buddhism means interdependence' (344). Cage sets up a

fundamental inseparableness between the self and language, a relationship which becomes the material site of emptiness, and which he calls 'poetry.' And he does not create a binary opposition between, on the one hand, language and the self and on the other hand emptiness, because that would mean setting up another duality, which is

of course contrary to Zen philosophy and experience. Nor does he negate the phenomenal world of language and subjectivity by positing a metaphysical realm of silent emptiness that stands outside of that world. Emptiness is not an other to the world, but it is the underlying condition of the world. Hence Cage can write in 'Lecture on Nothing'

that 'what we require is silence; but what silence requires is that I go on talking'

(109), thereby eliding the opposition between speech (the phenomenal world) and silence (the void, emptiness). Paradoxically, the subject of Cage's statement about

nothing is that which it is not – the 'I' is never present, because it resides in the language of nothing, which is empty and

nowhere. In the place of a separate and individual ego, a substantial 'something,' Cage's subject seems to negotiate a middle way between the personal self who can speak the word 'I,' and the wider horizon of language, nature and the phenomenal

world which are entirely vacant of self presence.

His 'I' says nothing, because it refuses to recognize itself as an autonomous individual, and recognizes instead its interdependent relationship with words, sounds, nature and ideas. ¶ Roughly contemporaneous with 'Lecture on Nothing' is Gaston Bachelard's 1958 text *The Poetics of Space*. Although Bachelard focuses primarily on the linguistic representation of space through imagery, we could extrapolate from his text to consider the non-linguistic, material performance of space and non-space – word and non-word, self and non-self –

as signifying events found in

Cage. Consider for example Bachelard's writing on poetic reverie or daydreaming as a form of transportation, 'outside the immediate world to a world that bears the mark of infinity' (183) – that is, the mark of a vast space which the poetic imagination

is able to enlarge indefinitely. To analyse this elsewhere is to enter 'into the purest form of phenomenology – a phenomenology without phenomena' (184). Since the immense is not an object *per se*, a 'phenomenology of the immense would refer us directly to our imagining consciousness' (184). Similarly, Cage's material

deployment of blank space and non-information points to the immensity of nothing, to the void which is for the Zen Buddhist an always already condition of existence. The void is at once vast, without time or space, as well as phenomenal, and fully formless.

Cage does not describe nature, the void, nothingness or the thematics of Zen, but offers instead a site

for direct experience, and for contemplating

the void which Zen posits as the ground of

all things, but which cannot be represented by conventional description. Extrapolating from Bachelard's words, the poet in this mode gives readers a sense that 'there is something

else to be expressed besides what is offered for objective expression' (186). Cage's 'spaced-out' texts deterritorialize the objective image, and substitute in its place the void of non-communication and non-identity.¶ Cage's 'I' in 'Lecture on Nothing' expresses a desire or

'need' to speak of nothing:
> I have nothing to say
> and I am saying it   and that is
> poetry   as I need it (*Silence* 109).

This need is not necessarily congruent with the Buddhist concept of craving, or *trsnā*, which is a blind grasping of the ego for 'the

illusion of something stable and permanent, substantial and unitary' (Miller 35). *Trsnā* can thus be differentiated from the sort of desire referred

to by the Buddha when he admonished his followers to 'cultivate a spontaneously overflowing *desire* for the well being of all' (Laycock 66). Instead of upholding the negative desire-as-lack scenario of *trsnā*, which seeks climax in the attainment of an object, Cage's 'Buddhist desire' follows a more positive route

by seeking to circulate and maintain itself as a paradoxical nothing. As N. Robert Glass points out, this form of desire is not dependent on objects, but sustains itself affectively through what Deleuze and Guattari

in *A Thousand*

Plateaus call a plateau or level of intensity. Buddhist experience is for Glass an intransitive force which requires going 'beyond desires dependent of sense objects' (69). From this angle, Cage's nothing is not without desire *per se*, but it is without the

negative desire-as-lack which strives to find fulfilment in objects.

This is not to say that the Buddhist teachings which have informed Cage ignore or despise sense objects, or that these teachings find those objects entirely illusory, but that both Buddhist

philosophy and Cagean poetics involve an acceptance of phenomena without the defilement of craving, thereby opening up a new space for the experience of things. ¶ During the late 1960s, Cage further developed his non-subjective approach by producing rule-driven poems which revolve around a kind of spine consisting of a proper name

or a found phrase. Cage originally thought of these poems as acrostics, but he soon came to call them 'mesostics' after his friend the philosopher Norman O. Brown pointed out

that the central spine of each poem was not situated at the left margin, as it would be in an acrostic poem, but down the middle. In one of his first published mesostic sequences, entitled '36 Mesostics

Re and not Re Marcel Duchamp' (1972), Cage uses his friend and mentor's name as a mesostic spine:

>   A utility aMong
>   swAllows
>   is theiR
>   musiC.
>   ThEy produce it mid-air
>   to avoid coLliding.
>
>   there is no Difference between life and death.
>   (sUzuki.)
>   it is Consistent
>   To say deatH is the most
>   importAnt thing one day and the next day
>   to say life is the Most
>   imPortant thing (*M* 26).

In these opening stanzas, the languages of Zen and of nature coalesce around Duchamp's

name. Cage links Duchamp, the Dada pioneer, to Suzuki, the Zen master; Suzuki as a metonymy for Zen is materially situated within the name of Duchamp, who is in turn a metonymy for the Dada impulse. The mesostic's 'wing words' (lines of horizontal text on each side of the poem's

spine), signify not only Suzuki's Zen teachings on the non-dualistic character of life and death, but also the music of nature, produced as utility by the swallows. By using Duchamp's name to signify both nature and Zen, Cage produces a text that is both about

and not about Marcel Duchamp – hence the poem's title. There is no difference, in the Zen view, between Duchamp, the sparrow's music, life and death. ¶ In composing the wing words of a mesostic, Cage typically trimmed his source text 'according to taste, limited, say to forty-three characters to the left and forty-three to the right' (Cage

'_____' 173). As Perloff points out, '*[c]hance operations*, even though the phrase is Cage's own, is a highly misleading term for what actually happens in a mesostic' (*Radical* 150). Given the predominance of non-intention in Cage's writing it seems

that his turn to personal taste is strangely uncharacteristic. While it is true to say that Cage made some subjective decisions in composing the precise length of his poems' horizontal lines,

he claimed that the non-intentional use of chance operations and the letters of the vertical string helped him out of sentimentality by giving him something to do, a puzzle to solve: 'I write or find a source text which is then used as an oracle [. . . .] This frees me from memory, tastes, likes and dislikes' (*I–VI* 1). And yet, Cage remained unclear about the precise rationale for his choice of wing words. Perloff sees this recourse to choice as a kind of Oulipian *clinamen* – that is, the introduction of spontaneity and the unexpected in the use of an ordered constraint. For all of its meticulous procedures, the mesostic's contradictory status as both non-intentional object and subjective compositional activity means that the poems oscillate between choice and choicelessness, purpose and purposelessness, and this oscillation moves the texts away from the subjective stance. In Buddhist terms, the mesostic presents a kind of 'middle way' between intention and non-intention, perhaps unwittingly paralleling the *Mādhyamaka* school of Buddhist thought articulated in the second- and third-century C.E. by Nāgārjuna, a philosopher who posited a middle ground between metaphysical views (for example, whether the self ultimately does or does not exist).[8] Cage's

mesostics articulate a fissure; on the one hand, his texts recognize the existence of a subject position – an identity situated in the social network, which can make choices according to taste, like and dislike. On the other hand, however, the mesostics are completely rule-bound, and these rules provide a means to diminish personal choice and self-identity. The resulting polarity is analogous

to Nāgārjuna's teachings about *śūnyatā-śūnyatā* (the emptiness of emptiness) because the poems avoid being completely attached to the void. Nāgārjuna cautions against becoming

attached to emptiness, and so the experience of *śūnyatā-śūnyatā* is of extreme importance to the Buddhist practitioner:

'[b]etter to be attached to a self as high as Mount Sumeru, than to be attached to the idea of *śūnyatā*' (qtd. in Sangarakshita *What* 84). If we consider Cage's chance operations as a means to silence the subjective ego in order to experience the greater silence of 'nothing' – that is, the void of non-dualistic 'interpenetration,' then Cage's turn to conditioned and subjective taste within the limits of chance operation provides a remedy to becoming attached to the unconditioned. ¶ For Cage, there is an

'incalculable infinity of causes and effects,' because everything in all of time and space is related to every other thing' (*Silence* 47). Here, Cage makes a reference to the notion of karma, a term which Buddhists often refer to as 'dependent origination' to indicate that nothing comes into being independently, but that all origins are dependent. The Buddhist view of karma is not

merely limited to the idea that a person's suffering or

happiness results from past actions. In other words, whatever objects do exist – be they organic or inorganic substances,

social situations, thoughts or emotions, or whatever – they have all come into their current form of existence because of many unknown causes. Dependent origination functions in a manner that is not entirely unlike the psychoanalytic concept of 'overdetermination,' a term which Freud coined in *The Interpretation of Dreams* to account for the fact that dreams are triggered by multiple causes. Dependent

origination is similarly overdetermined by numerous factors, although the Buddhist concept differs from psychoanalysis because it takes into account all of the innumerable causes contributing to a given situation, and it is not limited to psychological phenomenon. Moreover,

one

would have to be a fully enlightened Buddha to 'see' all of the causes of any given condition. Dependent origination provides an alternative way to describe the term *anātman* or 'no self.'

If everything has come into existence due to the overdetermination of unknown causes, how can anything be said to exist independently of those causes? ¶ Cage's writing on the overdetermined character of cause and effect, with its suggestion of a many-stranded 'interpenetration' of all things in time

and space, further suggests a subtle engagement with Buddhist ethics. The doctrine of dependent origination, with its stress on the overdetermination of cause and effect, implies that a person's present condition – their suffering or happiness – cannot be reduced to their own, individual actions. Our actions in the present will join with other factors to cause future results, and this cause and effect relationship is the basis for Buddhist ethics, sometimes summarized as 'actions have consequences'

(Sangharakshita *What* 165). Insight

into the law of karma is said by Buddhists to sweep away the delusion that the self is a separate entity, and Buddhist philosophy maintains that freedom from suffering arises when this delusion is overcome. The resulting 'Great Death' of the conditioned ego leads to

a tremendous transformation in consciousness, from suffering and selfishness to liberation and compassion. That this transformation results in compassion is evidenced by the first of the four Bodhisattva aspirations, which are recited daily in Zen monasteries and temples: '[a]ll beings, without

number, I vow to liberate.' For Buddhists, the law of causality informs

the ethical sphere, and Cage's writing on causation follows suit. Where the Buddhist develops a sense of mindfulness about the emptiness of karmic formations, Cage advocates a form of mindful aesthetic practice – one that is not based on self-expression or on grasping after identity, but on increasing the awareness of impermanence and suchness. And when Cage writes that 'the

highest purpose is to have no purpose' and stresses the importance of identifying with 'what is here and now' (*Silence* 155), the thought could

be reconsidered in Buddhist terms as an active portrayal of mindfulness practice, in which 'karmic formations are allowed to rise into the mind and then to pass into cessation – *without being acted upon*' (Snelling 71). Mindfulness of the empty, impermanent character of phenomenon weakens karmic formations, thereby bringing the observer closer to the

ultimately compassionate, wisdom-filled character of enlightenment. In the Mahāyāna context which informs Zen experience, and which is foundational for Cage's Zen poetics, mindful awareness and compassion are hallmarks of the Bodhisattva ideal. ¶ What becomes apparent in Cage's performative use of empty space is his deep affinity with the Buddhist concept of *śūnyatā*.

Emptiness is merely a linguistic term for the insight that the phenomenal world is tied together in a non-dualistic, interrelated web, in which no single phenomenon stands alone. The void is not an absence, but the ground of all things, including the self and nature. For Buddhist commentator Michael Adam, emptiness reveals the 'many things [. . .] by showing itself as them [. . . .] All things are One and that

is No-thing' (45). Buddhist literature often refers to the 'many things' cited by Adam as the 'ten thousand'[9] or the 'myriad' things; Dōgen Zenji, the thirteenth-century founder of the Sōtō Zen school, taught his students that: '[t]o

study the Buddha Way is to study the self. To study the self is to forget the self. To forget the self is to be actualized by myriad things' (71). Cage's turn towards non-intentional composition and poetics perfectly models

the inter-relationship between the self and the myriad things: 'this psychological turning leads to the world of nature, where, gradually or suddenly, one sees

that humanity and nature, not separate, are in this world together; that

nothing was lost when everything was given away' (*Silence* 8).

THE IMITATION OF NATURE IN HER MANNER OF OPERATION 49

In other words, when the ego is realized as nothing, an object 'given away,' the inseparable character of humanity and nature becomes evident. ¶ The contradiction between losing nothing while giving everything away bears some resemblance to the Zen practice of 'letting go' during meditation. Paul Williams writes that when the meditator sees that 'things are

sources of unhappiness, out of one's control, and impermanent [. . .] one lets them go' (*Buddhist* 60). The word Zen is a Japanese derivative of the Chinese word *Chàn*, which is in turn a translation of the Sanskrit word *dhyana*, or meditation. In effect, Zen is the 'meditation' school of Buddhism; although all Buddhist schools stress the

importance of mediation, Zen training places the utmost importance on sitting meditation, which it calls *zazen*. To practice *zazen* is to let go, to 'give up everything around us' and to 'discard all that is connected with our sense organs and intellect' (Yamada 8). The practitioner of

zazen is urged

to let go of the intellect and the

emotions, the everyday world of social relations, and the egoic self. The result of extended *zazen* practice is

a transformation of the mind, which eventually leads to the end of suffering and the attainment of liberation. However, Cage's letting go does not occur in the context of

a regular practice of *zazen*; while he attended Suzuki's classes in Zen Buddhist philosophy at Columbia University[10] and was generally steeped in the Zen literature available to Western students at

the time, Cage claims that he 'never practiced sitting cross-legged,' and that he did not meditate ('Where' 43). Here Cage resembles Thomas Cleary's characterization of Suiwō, an eccentric Zen teacher who often spoke outside the bounds of normal conversation, hardly sat in meditation at all,

scarcely read any scripture, enjoyed chess (in Cage's case, with Marcel Duchamp) and lived life as he pleased (49). In Zen, meditation is not only reserved for special occasions, but any activity or circumstance offers the student an opportunity for mindful, meditative practice.

Exercise in mindful awareness is especially true for the traditional Zen arts, and Watts points out that such Zen-inspired arts as *sumi* painting or *haiku* poetry do not absolutely require the specific sitting technique of *zazen*. What they do require, however, is a 'total presence of mind' leading to the 'instantaneous awakening' of *satori* (Watts *Way* 218). Cage's lack of formal *zazen* practice in favour of an aesthetic activity which reflects in

his 'engagement in Zen' (*Silence* ix) shares a similar inspiration. His frequent reiterations of emptiness, indeterminacy and spontaneity imply that his writing exemplifies not only the experimental tradition of twentieth-century poetics, but also the on-going tradition of Zen aesthetics. *Silence* offers readers a key site for the development of Zen-based arts, because it expands the range of possibilities for Zen

aesthetics, and moves them beyond the largely tradition-bound constraints of their Japanese background. Here Cage's emphasis on experimental form resonates with a Zen maxim quoted by Suzuki: 'to point at the moon, a finger

is needed, but woe to those who take the finger for the moon' (*Essays* 19). This statement cautions Zen students to distinguish between, on the one hand, words or objects of art which signify Buddhist enlightenment, and on the other

hand, the direct experience of enlightenment itself. To risk rehearsing a Buddhist cliché, one could say that Cage's non-traditional approach to Zen aesthetics echoes the seventeenth-century haiku master and Zen student Matsuo Basho's advice to avoid following 'in the footsteps of the wise' – that is, to dispense with traditional thought and practice – in favour of seeking 'what they sought' (1). ¶ For someone with such an overt interest in writing and Zen, Cage rarely quotes

Buddhist scripture, preferring instead to draw on Suzuki, Watts and other

secondary sources. An anonymous verse from T'ang dynasty China describes *Chàn* Buddhism as a 'special transmission outside the scriptures,'

with 'no dependence on words and letters,'[11] and Cage's lack of reliance on canonical Buddhist texts implies a similar form of iconoclasm. It is not that the early *Chàn* and Zen

masters disagreed with the scriptural authorities; monks chanted sutras daily and probably had many of them memorized. However, Zen does not rely on words alone, because words convey ideas about an experience rather than the experience itself. Paradoxically, this form of non-linguistic practice is precisely the experience that Cage's poetics seek to encounter. But instead of meditation and the disciplined study of scriptures, Cage used writing, music, visual art and other forms of cultural production to form a type of meditative engagement with 'silence,' which he regarded as a 'ground, so to speak, in which emptiness could grow' ('Where' 43). ¶ Cage's silence seems to legitimate nature

over scripture; although Cage was seldom direct in acknowledging the South-Asian philosopher Ananda Coomaraswamy's influence on his own writing, he frequently quoted Coomaraswamy's definition of art as 'the imitation of Nature in her manner of operation.' Cage read Coomaraswamy's *The Transformation of Nature in Art* (1934)

shortly after his arrival in New York in 1942 – a few years before his encounters with Suzuki. What did he learn from this text? David W. Patterson points out that Coomaraswamy's view of nature owes much to Thomas Aquinas, who applied the term 'Nature' to the broadest context, 'indicating the universal, natural order through

which individual phenomena is created' (195). Coomaraswamy further alludes to the Buddhist philosopher Hseih Ho's assertion that art must reveal 'the operation of the spirit (*ch'i*) in life-movement' (qtd. in Patterson 196). There are, however, significant differences between Cage and Coomaraswamy; while Coomaraswamy stresses the importance of subject matter, clear expression and effective communication (Patterson 197), Cage dismisses both subject matter and lucid communication:

'[t]here is no communication and nothing being said' (*Year* 101).¹² ¶ Cage's 1961 essay

'On Robert Rauschenberg, Artist and

his Work' centres on the painter's capacity to 'unfocus attention' through two devices: on one hand, Rauschenberg employs symmetrical composition, which Cage finds to be uninteresting and 'nothing special,' and on the other hand, Rauschenberg uses an

'over-

all' compositional method, 'where each small part is a sample of what you find elsewhere' (*Silence* 100). Cage situates his discussion

of Rauschenberg's compositional practices immediately before his citation of Coomaraswamy, perhaps suggesting that the painter's work exemplifies Coomaraswamy's definition of art as an imitation of natural process, in which art and nature function analogously in their manner of operation. Cage further writes in the Rauschenberg essay that art is the imitation of nature 'or a net' (*Silence* 100). 'Indra's Net,' writes Stephen Batchelor, is 'a vast grid of interconnected mirroring spheres, each one reflecting all the others' (35). The third-century CE *Avatamsaka Sutra*, or the 'Flower Adornment' sutra, employs the 'Jewelled Net of Indra' as a metaphor for interdependence. This teaching

was fully developed in China by the *Hua-yen* school during the sixth century, and then

later transmitted to Japan under the Japanese name *Kegon*. Tu Shun, a patriarch of the *Hua-yen* school, explains the metaphor as a net made of jewels, which 'reflect each other's images, appearing in each other's reflections upon reflections, *ad infinitum*

[. . .] in one jewel there are all the jewels' (66). Martine Batchelor glosses this passage: '[i]n this way Chinese Buddhists realized how

all things are intimately connected with each other. They call this the doctrine of the "mutual interpenetration and interfusion of all phenomena"' (11). *Hua-yen/Kegon* maintain that the Buddha preached the *Avatamsaka* immediately after his enlightenment, but that at that time his hearers were not yet ready to understand it. For this reason, he evolved the

less complex teachings (collected as the Theravada scriptures), which circulated until his followers were ready to understand the *Avatamsaka*. The sutra thus remains for *Hua Yen/Kegon* the 'summation and apogee of [the Buddha's] system' (Snelling 152). Suzuki had the highest respect for the teachings of the *Avatamsaka*, and taught it to his classes at Columbia. Moreover, the philosophy of interpenetration significantly

influenced the Zen tradition, where it found a less 'abstract expression' (Batchelor 12). Instead of the cosmic metaphor of an infinite network of jewels spread out by the Vedic god Indra, in which no phenomenon

stands on its own and all things are dependent on all other things, Zen points at the ordinary things of the world – the 'myriad' things of everyday reality – and finds in them the same form of interdependence. And it is precisely this form of holographic, infinite interdependency that Cage finds in Rauschenberg's 'all-over' compositional method. Where Tu Shun writes,

'[i]f you sit in

one jewel, then you are sitting in all jewels in every direction, multiplied over and over' (66), Cage writes, 'each small part is a sample of what you find elsewhere' (*Silence* 100). As a compositional method, the all-over net is also employed by Cage, for in the introductory head note to his essay on Rauschenberg, he writes that the lecture 'may be

read in whole or in part; any sections of it may be skipped, what remains may be read

in any order' (*Silence* 98). Much like the metaphor of the net, in which 'there is no going or coming' (Tu Shun 66), Cage's compositional method offers readers no place of origin, no continuous narrative, no logical argument, and no teleological conclusion. ¶ When questioned during the late 1960s

about cultivating indifference to individual, subjective emotions, Cage replied 'we must consider *ecology* even more than the individual,' and our ecological and social

problems could be solved by 'reintegrating

individuals into nature (*For* 56)'. He further advocates taking responsibility for 'any being, living or not'. Or as the Buddhists put it: 'for all beings, sentient and non-sentient' (*For* 97). Here Cage has in mind the Buddhist levelling of differences between subject and object, culture and nature, the sentient and the non-sentient. William Grosnick comments that in the moment of realization, 'a

Buddha does not see a distinction between himself and the grasses, trees or land that surround him, those grasses and trees and that land all "become" him, which is to say they

"become Buddha"' (206). Or as Zen master Dōgen puts

it: 'The green mountains are neither sentient

being nor non-sentient being. One's own self is neither sentient nor non-sentient being' (qtd. in Grosnick 204). Suzuki's version of Zen accords with this non-dualistic ecological perspective;

as Ian Harris points out, Suzuki was one of the earliest writers to have articulated to a

western readership the position that Buddhism is eco-friendly.[13] Cage's writing on ecology and his ecological approach to writing can be understood in this non-dualistic context. His call for a reintegration of individuals into the net of nature is based on the Zen understanding that human beings and nature are indistinguishable: both nature and culture are fundamentally empty of self, impermanent forms of 'nothing,' silent examples of Buddhist mind: 'birth, death, coming and

going are mind; years, months, days and hours are mind; dreams, mirages, and sky-flowers are mind; splashes, bubbles, and flames are mind [. . .].' (Dōgen qtd. in

Grosnick 206). ¶ The rampant piling up of recycled textual information in Cage's work rehearses the same type of undecidability of meaning that we find in his indeterminate, *kōan*-like stories,

although in this case indeterminacy does not occur because of puzzling narratives which represent an event 'outside'

of the text, but from the extreme 'noise' of Cage's linguistic material. *Empty Words*

and other texts by Cage do not tell us stories or relate events or even reflect on themes. Instead they offer an overload of non-semantic nothingness, a flattening out of conceptual logic. For Jeff Hilson, many works written within the tradition of formally innovative poetics produce what might be called a 'lo-fi' textual experience (103). Hilson

draws on R. Murray Schafer's writing about recorded music in order to distinguish between the 'favourable signal to noise ratio' of hi-fi recordings, and the obscure, over-dense 'population of sounds' found in low-fi recordings (43). Cage's writing, with its

super abundance of textual noise, perfectly models Hilson's analogy between lo-fi music and formally innovative poetics. *Empty Words* maintains a sense of semantic opacity, in which no single word, image, or concept can be heard above the silence and/or the din of the whole. In Buddhist terms, the resulting lo-fi text models the interdependent character of phenomena,

in

which no discrete object can stand alone, or be grasped as a separate entity. ¶ It may be enlightening to contrast Cage's

lo-fi approach to Buddhist poetics and his view of nature with the most culturally prominent

of contemporary Buddhist 'ecopoets,' Gary Snyder. 'This living flowing land / Is all there is,' writes Snyder in 'By Frazier Creek Falls'

(1974), 'We *are* it / It sings through us' (477). Here Snyder typically self-identifies with nature, claiming that

we 'are' the land, thereby voicing a non-dualistic, deep-ecological continuum between nature and culture.[14] Terry Gifford writes that this passage is characteristic of Snyder's attempt to heal

our culture's dualistic estrangement from nature, to 'reconnect our culture with the wider ecosystem' (83). The theme of non-dualism, which owes much to Snyder's Zen

Buddhist practice, is undoubtedly central to his writing. Following Hilson's terms, we could say that Snyder's text is a piece of 'hi-fi' poetry, because unlike Cage's writing it produces very little noise. In Snyder's poem, the ratio between signal (sense) and noise (non-sense) is favourable – that is, the poem minimizes non-signifying interference in order to economically transmit its thematic signal. However, although Snyder

explores the theme of non-dualism, his work does not question the dualistic barrier between subject and object – or between signifier and signified – at the formal, linguistic level. Regardless of Snyder's level of Zen experience, his text remains a dualistic re-presentation of that experience. This is a problem with the communicative function of language itself, inasmuch as language distorts reality

by separating and labelling the world into disparate bits. The word 'land' employed by Snyder, for example, is not the land itself, but a sound image, something that stands in for the object and/or mental concept that English labels the 'land.' Early Buddhist philosophy recognized the impossibility of communicating 'truth' in language, and developed the so-

called 'two-truth' doctrine in order to articulate the difference between relative, every-day language and the language used to express the ultimate truth of emptiness. On the one hand, conventional truth(*samvṛtisatya*) articulates common-sense knowledge about the way things are. If I say that my

name is John and that I live in the USA and

that I have such-and-such a passport number, I am speaking conventional truth. On the other hand, absolute truth (*paramārthasatya*) articulates the way things really are: 'empty, beyond thought and description' (Snelling 102). Snyder's approach is closer to conventional truth, because he employs language to communicate about the theme of non-dualism; in this respect he is similar to the Buddhist teacher who employs conventional truth in order to lead

his students towards enlightenment. Many of Cage's explanatory notes for lectures follow this approach. However, his linguistically indeterminate,

chance-based work seems closer to this second, absolute approach to truth, because it does not attempt to describe its referent or to communicate a conceptual 'meaning' about nature or language. By presenting a glut of textual information, Cage

rearticulates information as loss, and cancels the act of description in favour of a direct engagement with 'empty' linguistic noise. And it is this *direct* presentation of the thing itself – in the form of linguistic materiality and in the spatialized fabric of silence itself – that distinguishes Cage's work from texts which dualistically foreground the *themes* of Buddhism, nature, the self, silence or any other mental concept. Unlike

Snyder and many of his

other contemporaries with an interest in Buddhism, Cage usually refuses to recycle explicit references to Buddhism or to any form of literal Buddhist content. Nor does he make reference to personal identity, unless it

is to negate that identity, disposing it among the excessive accretion of linguistic detritus which constitutes so much of his writing, and which in every case is recycled from

earlier textual sources. ¶ 'The more information you have, the higher degree of entropy, so that one piece of information tends to cancel out the other' (Smithson 302). Ecopoet and critic

Jonathan Skinner has borrowed the term *entropological* poetics from land artist and writer Robert Smithson, in order to describe a formal practice engaging with 'the level of materials and processes, where entropy, transformation and decay

are part of the creative work,' and focusing primarily on the 'procedures and materiality of the letter' ('Statement' 128). Entropological writers listed by Skinner in this group include Ian Hamilton Finlay, John Cayley and John Cage.[15] Although Skinner does not develop his thoughts about Cage in great detail, he draws on Smithson's explanation of entropology as

a means to indicate highly developed poetic structures in a state of disintegration. For

Smithson, entropology occurs when information 'obliterates itself so that there is obviously information there, but the information is so overwhelming in terms of its physicality that it tends to lose itself' (219). One could say that entropological poetics use language

to collaborate with the physical, material dynamics of entropy found in nature, thereby creating a non-dualistic relationship between language and the natural world. Of course, in Buddhist terms the materiality of nature considered by Skinner is also empty of substantial being. The Mahāyāna scriptures declare

that '[v]oidness does not result from the destruction of matter, but

the nature of matter is itself voidness. Therefore, to speak of voidness on the one hand, and of matter [. . .] on the other – is entirely dualistic' (Thurman 74-5). If, as Thurman points out, Mahāyāna

philosophy considers our immediate reality to be 'the ultimate, perfect reality' where 'matter is voidness' (3), then it is the job of the Buddhist to accept that reality as it is, and not to strive towards escaping the imperfection of the world for a hypostatized world of otherness. With this perspective in mind, we could rephrase the *Heart Sutra*'s claim that emptiness does not differ from form, and that form does not differ from emptiness, as *nature* does not differ from void, and void does not differ from nature. Or in terms more sympathetic to the specifics of

Cage's early lectures, language does not differ from silence, and silence does not differ from language. Perhaps Cage's most sustained

engagement with entropological language occurs in his various intertextual rewritings of nineteenth-century American philosopher and writer Henry David Thoreau, whose work on the relationship between social conditions and nature anticipated

many contemporary environmentalist concerns.[16] In 1967, Wendell Berry introduced Cage to Thoreau's *Journal* (1858), and Cage writes that at that time he was 'starved

for Thoreau' (*Empty* 11) and that in reading Thoreau's *Journal* he discovered 'any idea I've ever had worth its salt' (*Empty* 4). Cage produced several texts based on Thoreau's writing, including *Mureau* (1970), the title of which comes from condensing the words *music* and

Thoreau, and 'Lecture on the Weather' (1975), a musical composition which samples passages drawn from Thoreau's writing. *Mureau* recycles[17] letters, syllables, phrases and complete sentences drawn from Thoreau's *Journal*; Cage wrote it by 'subjecting all the remarks of Henry David Thoreau about music, silence and sounds he heard that are indexed in the Dover

publication of the *Journal* to a series of *I Ching* chance operations' (*M* ix). Thoreau in Cage's hands becomes a metonymy for natural processes, in which the treated text is a material thing, another element in the field of nature. Free from the dualistic reflection on nature which characterizes so much traditional 'nature poetry' and which separates the reader from

the text and the text from the world, *Mureau* offers readers no means to ontologically ground their subjectivity in opposition to the

representation of

nature:

> sparrowssitA g**RO**sbeak betrays i*tself*by that peculiarsq**ueaka- riEFFECT OF SLIGHTE**st tinkling measures soundness ingpleasa**We hear!** Does it not rather hear us?**sWhen he hears** the telegraph, he thinksthose bugs have issu*e*d forthThe Owl wakes to*u*ches the stops, wakes reverberations *d gwalky* In verse there is no inherent *music eo*fsttakestakes a man to make a room silent [. . .] (*M* 35).

The various fonts, word fragments, unorthodox spacings and non-uniform type-faces of Cage's entropological nature writing call attention to linguistic materiality, and muddle

the clear transmission of information. One could say that his texts' foregrounding of semantic loss serves as a linguistic analogy to the Second

Law of Thermodynamics, in which energy is more easily lost than obtained, being transformed into 'an all-encompassing sameness' (Smithson 11).[18] We could recast Smithson's all-encompassing

sameness in a Zen context by pointing to the Buddhist faith in the non-dualistic character of phenomena. Suzuki explains that the mind which 'functions with nature' is no longer harassed by dualistic thoughts (*Zen* 118), and that by realizing the 'One Mind' of the Buddha, the Zen student finds no distinction between self and

other, nature and culture. As Huang-Po writes, '[y]ou should know that there is One Mind only, and besides this there is not an atom of anything you can claim to be your own' (qtd. in Suzuki *Zen* 131). Cage's propensity to

overload the reader with a glut of textual information leads to a similar condition of non-dualistic equilibrium, in which no single element stands out, and in which there is no fixed focus or

identity between subject and object. ¶ As Cage reminds us again and again in his early lectures, his work is not to be taken as a preconceived aesthetic object or as

site for conceptual reasoning, but as an occasion for lived experience (*Silence* 31). His entropological poetics reduce the traditionally dominant position of culture over nature, and suggest instead a belief in the mutual interaction and interdependence of nature and culture. One effect of this equilibrium is a lessening

of intention. Not only does Cage draw on Coomaraswamy's writing to consider art to be the 'imitation of nature in her manner of operation' (*Silence* 100), but he also claims that the 'highest purpose is to have no purpose / at all,' and that the purposeful lack of purpose again puts one in 'accord with nature in her manner of operation' (*Silence* 155). Cage here links Coomaraswamy's writing on art with what Watts describes as the Zen stilling of all mental discrimination in order

to experience the world as unclassified suchness, to awaken compassion (*karuna*), and to 'become consciously identified with the playful and purposeless character of the void' (*Way* 96). Watts further

writes that the Zen life is 'completely aimless' (166), and he argues that when there is no goal the 'human senses are fully open to receive the world' (195). Given Cage's interest in Watts writing on Zen, it should come as no surprise that Watts's words on Buddhist aimlessness resonate so clearly with Cage's

continual stress on non-intention. ¶ 'My work was only sometimes that of identifying, as Duchamp had, found objects' (Cage *Writings* n.p.).For Kenneth Goldsmith, Cage's influence as composer, poet and philosopher from the 1940s to the early 1990s 'cannot be underestimated' ('Why' xx). Indeed, Cage's impersonal and procedural poetics provide a significant

precursor to the conceptual art practice of the 1960s, with its re-definition of the art object and its reconfiguration of the role of viewers into active participants in the creation of meaning. Moreover,

Cage's Duchampian 'recycling' of found material was continued by various conceptualists during the 1960s.[19] Joseph Kosuth's

Purloined: A Novel (1967–2000), for example, is composed entirely from photocopies of pages taken from other books and compiled to form a single book, while Vito Acconci's 'Contacts/Contexts (Frame of Reference)' (1969) consists of verbatim passages taken directly from Roget's *Thesaurus*. The early conceptualist challenge to the dominant cultural assumption of

art as a vehicle for personal expression was foreshadowed by Cage, because his working methods were completely at odds with the notion that art must express

subjectivity. However, where the conceptualists sought to step away

from personal expression in order to investigate the role of the aesthetic object in various institutional contexts or to present language itself as an artwork,[20] Cage's limitation of personal expression and use of found text grow out of his understanding of

Buddhist *śūnyatā*, and his work is unintelligible without taking this crucial understanding into account. ¶ In the context of American writing during the 1950s and 1960s, prominent examples of found or recycled poetry include Olson's sporadic use of collage elements drawn from letters

and historical accounts in *The Maximus Poems* (1960), and John Ashbery's early book *The Tennis Court Oath* (1962). As Andrew Ross notes, Ashbery

used collage and 'the intrusion or intervention of found material to break up

the purified realm of the poem'

(209). Perhaps more pertinent in this context is Ted Berrigan's 'An Interview with John Cage' (1966), a text which spuriously

attributes Cage with the words of

Andy Warhol, William S. Burroughs and others; Cage permitted the publication of this text in the journal *Mother* 7 with a disclaimer stating that he served neither as collaborator nor interviewee (Dworkin *Against* 105). Berrigan's most celebrated work, *The Sonnets* (1964), frequently recycles textual material drawn from other writing, including, most notably, language drawn from Shakespeare's sonnets as well as from Arthur Rimbaud, Dick

Gallup, John Ashbery, Joe Brainard (to whom the book is dedicated), Charles Olson, and Edgar Rice Burroughs. Berrigan once told students: 'if you can't think of any terrific lines, just take them from other poets' ('Business' 44). More recent use of found material occurs in the work of conceptual writers such as Vanessa Place and Robert Fitterman,

and Cage's recycling of

textual material seems to straddle their method and the early collage-like cut ups of Ashbery and Berrigan. Fitterman is clear about the difference between the conceptual writer as 'plagiarist' and this earlier approach; where the collagist brings 'appropriated materials together [. . .] to a singular expression,'

the plagiarist presents source material in large, unmodified

chunks

such as a whole paragraph or even an entire page lifted directly from a book, thereby reframing works that already exist 'in new contexts

to give them new meanings' (15). Cage's appropriation of source texts is 'plagiarist' in Fitterman's sense to the extent that it frequently draws from single texts, such as Thoreau's *Journal* or Joyce's

Finnegans Wake, rather than collaging together language from a number of different texts. However, Cage does not strictly adhere to the conceptual plagiarist's use of unmodified textual material, for his 'writing-

through' of source texts entails recycling them in an altered form; for all his indebtedness to Duchamp and the readymade art object, Cage's use of chance operations modifies them beyond the scope of recontextualization. ¶ Sol LeWitt's 'Paragraphs on Conceptual Art,' (1967) illustrates how conceptual art of the 1960s prioritized idea over material form. LeWitt dismisses the art object as a secondary

afterthought: 'when an artist uses a conceptual form of art' he writes, 'it means that

all of the planning and decisions are

made beforehand and the execution is a perfunctory affair. The idea is a machine that makes the art' (5). Shortly after LeWitt's article was published, Lucy Lippard coined the now well-known phrase 'the dematerialization of

the art object' (6), in order to emphasize the importance of the art idea as opposed to the documentation of that idea through language, photography, or another

medium. One significant outcome of this dematerialization is the critique that it offers to socially reified assumptions about value – that is, dematerialization calls into question the cultural legitimation of art or text as *product*, as commodity. Instead dematerialization foregrounds the *process* of the art work's creation, and re-situates art as research on the social and aesthetic

conditions of its own production. While Cage's work shows some affinity to conceptualism due to its use of impersonal compositional methods, Cage took issue with conceptual art's stress on dematerialization. Daniel Charles points out that several conceptualists viewed Cage's practice favourably, because works such as his silent piece *4'33'* demonstrate the notion that nothing may remain of the art object but the idea or concept (*For* 152–3). Yet Cage disagrees strongly with this form of dematerialization, because it 'obliges us to imagine that we know something *before* that something has happened. That is difficult, because the experience is always different from what you thought about it' (*For* 153). This stress on experience over preconceived idea could

of course be re-cast as a Zen-inspired critique of the ego's fixation on logic and rationality rather than on a direct encounter with phenomena. Cage does not overtly bring Zen philosophy to bear on his discussion of conceptualism, nonetheless,

his response to conceptual art remains clearly motivated by Zen: silence is not the same as the idea of silence, and dematerialization does not equal emptiness.¶ 'Clearly we are be- / ginning to get / nowhere' (*Silence* 114). In 1949, Cage delivered his 'Lecture on Nothing' at the Artists' Club

in New York. This lecture employed the same form of rhythmic structures that Cage used in his musical compositions at the time, and included fourteen repetitions of the refrain 'If anyone is sleepy let him go to sleep.' The lecture concluded with a question period, in which Cage gave one of six previously prepared answers regardless of the question, claiming

that his approach reflected his engagement with Zen (*Silence* ix). How does the tedium of these repetitions, which caused one audience member to scream that she could not 'bear another minute' while leaving part way through the performance, engage with Zen Buddhism? Williams comments that Western readers

of the Mahāyāna sutras often find them to be boring because the sutras conflate and expand time, miss

logical connections, move rapidly between ideas which are so compressed and arcane that they appear to be meaningless, and include page after page of repetition (*Mahāyāna* 37). This description might also be applied to Cage's writings, which could never be characterized as easily consumable page turners. The Zen monastery is similarly a place of repetition and regular, seemingly monotonous patterns of behaviour. Monks

sit in *zazen*, practice *kinhin* (walking meditation), eat, clean their bowls, sit in *zazen* again, and so on. There is very little scope in the monastic situation for anything other than mindfulness, and the Zen practitioner uses the monastery's lack of excitement as a tool to further their practice. ¶ Cage experimented further with boredom and attention

with a reading of *Empty Words* (1975) at the Naropa Institute in Boulder, Colorado, as part of the Institute's

Jack Kerouac School of Disembodied Poetics summer programme. This privately-run writing programme was set up according to Buddhist principles in 1974 by the Tibetan *Rinpoche* Chögyam Trungpa and the poets Allen Ginsberg and Anne Waldman. The entirety of *Empty Words* was intended to last 10 hours in performance,

with a half hour break between each section, although Cage decided to limit his reading to the final, 2-hour long section of the text for his Naropa performance. The

reading was also accompanied by reproductions of Thoreau's drawings, projected onto a screen in the auditorium where Cage read. In composing *Empty Words*, Cage recycled a source text by subjecting Thoreau's *Journal* to chance operations, and then re-recycled that source with more chance operations in order to develop the next version,

and so on. So the fragmented and de-composed bits of words in the latter sections do not draw directly on Thoreau, but on other versions of the *Journals* which Cage also created in the process of

writing the poem. *Empty Words* thus consists of a text which refers to another text which also refers to other texts in an on-going and potentially limitless process. By foregrounding

the interdependency of signifiers over the transfer of signified meaning, Cage celebrates the materiality of the signifier itself, at the level of the letter and the phoneme – a celebration which Cage called a 'transition from language to

music (a language already without sentences, and not confined to any subject [. . .])' (*Empty* 65). At Naropa, Cage read in a non-expressive monotone from the final section of *Empty Words*,

and punctuated his reading with long periods of silence:
            [. . .] m   ax
        ofi
    eo   llsth   tlgr nr
    pnscc
                u   tl th
                rk

    rmn   ei

            dryf m s n l s rpr rstwe rd oo g we [. . .] (68).

Given the Buddhist

foundation of Naropa, Cage thought the setting was appropriate, and he presented the lecture while sitting on stage with his back to the audience – a performative reference to the

story of Bodhidharma, the fifth-century C.E. Indian monk and first Chinese patriarch of Zen. It is said that Bodhidharma sat in silent mediation facing the rock wall of a cave in China for nine years; Cage's performance lasted for over two and a half hours. He read in a steady, meditative manner for the duration of the performance, because he

believed that this quality 'would be appreciated in a Buddhist situation' (Kostelanetz 132). The audience reacted by throwing objects at the stage, playing the guitar, making bird whistles and screaming, while Allen Ginsberg and other friendly listeners formed a circle around Cage for his protection (Silverman 266). Cage then pointed

out to the audience that they were not engaging in honest critique but were reacting emotionally (rather than mindfully) against boredom, a mental state which he claimed 'comes not from without

but from within' ('John' 220). *Empty Words* speaks 'nothing,' and its inscription of a space for spacelessness registers affectively on the audience as boredom. What is significant here in terms of Cage's approach to Buddhist practice is his suggestion that boredom provides a welcome state for the development of concentration, and for progress on the Buddhist path. This notion is widely accepted in all schools of Buddhist meditation, and especially in Zen as it is practised in the West, because Western culture is so heavily focussed on the desire for excitement. The mindful awareness of boredom provides a strong antidote to that desire.[21] For instance, when a Western Zen student complained to her teacher that the hours she spent sitting during *sesshin* (retreat) led her mainly to boredom, her teacher laughed and told her to be mindful of the boredom, and to note it with the words 'bored, bored, bored' until it vanished. Much to her surprise this technique worked – by noting the experience of boredom mindfully rather than reacting against it, the experience eventually shifted (Kapleau 286). Cage's non-signifying, entropological poetics resonate with this practice, and Cage recommends

a similar noting of

boredom: '[i]f something is boring after two minutes, try it for four. If still boring, then eight. Then sixteen. Then thirty-two. Eventually one discovers that it is not boring at all' (*Silence* 93). Another Cagean equation: 'Boredom + Attention = Becoming Interested' (*Composition* 58). Here the mindful acknowledgement (and embrace) of boredom allows one to shift into a more

positive mental state. ¶ When Cage cites Zen as a pretext for mindfully examining

the mental state of boredom, and claims that there is 'no more boredom as soon as there is no more ego' (*For* 49), he rehearses the Buddhist experience of letting go of self and the delusional mental states and perceptions that help to constitute that

self. How does Buddhism typically consider

the relationship between mental state and perception? Buddhist philosophy posits six sense faculties or *indriyas* for human beings: along with sight, hearing, touch, smell and taste the Buddhist subject is endowed with the sense faculty of mind (*manas*), which senses thoughts and ideas in the same way that the ear hears sounds or

the eye senses light.

These faculties come into contact with the conditioned world, and give

rise to feelings of pleasure, pain or neutrality. To experience the pain of boredom is to reside in the world of dualities, to discriminate between excitement and boredom, and to consequently desire that appears to be

entertaining. This conditioned pathway occurs precisely because the mind perceives phenomena as

if they were separate, individually existing entities and the mind consequently grasps at cause and effect: if I leave this reading or put down this book, I

won't be bored. ¶ Goldsmith has coined the term 'unboring boring' to indicate a kind of boredom which is 'fascinating, engrossing, transcendent and downright sexy' (68). 'Unboring boring is a voluntary state,' writes Goldsmith,

'the sort of boredom that we surrender ourselves to when, say, we go to see a piece of minimalist music' (68). Surrendering to the unboring boring appears to be a crucial practice, both for the audience

of much of the neo-avant-garde work of the 1960s and 1970s, and for the practitioner of Zen, who voluntarily undertakes the discipline of just sitting and watching the mind without recourse to excitement or distraction. Notably, Cage's work bridges these two separate pursuits by suggesting that aesthetic work can function as a form of meditation – that is, as a

vehicle for mindful awareness. What I find significant here is Cage's disciplined inscription of chaos. His work often is prefaced by detailed instructions on precisely how it should be

performed; 'Lecture on Nothing,' for example, includes an

introductory note stating that the text's four columns should be read from left to right rather than from top to bottom, and that the reading should also not be performed in an artificial manner, but with the *rubato* of everyday speech (109). In the 'Communication' section

of 'Composition as Process,' Cage likewise includes the statement that he always prescribes a 'performance timing' before delivering the lecture (41). On one hand, it seems that Cage's rigorous directions are superfluous: if it is Cage's intention to let things be as they are and to experience the chaos

of phenomena as it is, then why construct such an elaborate set

of directions for experiencing that chaos? Here it is useful to compare

Cage's disciplined approach to the discipline of Zen. Ultimately, all of the rituals, doctrines and experiences of Zen are seen by its adherents as being empty. They exist as disciplines simply in order to help the aspirant to attain insight into that emptiness – that is, as

forms of

'skill in means' leading the Zen trainee towards an experience of *śūnyatā*. Given the Zen underpinnings of Cage's poetics, is it not likely that his disciplined performance directions were intended to provide his

audience and readers with a similar encounter with the void, at least to the extent that Cage himself had experienced such an encounter? ¶ By way of comparison with Cage's disciplined approach to composition, consider the more expressive, speech-based Buddhist poetics of Allen Ginsberg, especially since 1970 and his association with the teachings of the Tibetan Lama Chögyam Trungpa. Ginsberg read

Buddhist and Hindu texts and studied with various Tibetan Buddhist teachers, Zen masters and Hindu swamis, but in 1970 he met Trungpa, and he began studying with him exclusively in 1971. Trungpa asked Ginsberg why he depended on a piece of paper when he recited his poetry, and he advised Ginsberg to

try improvising spontaneously in performance, without recourse to a previously written text. Ginsberg

responded by performing without books

or texts at a 1971 benefit reading for Tarthang Tulku's Tibetan Buddhist meditation centre in Berkley, where he chanted the *Padma Sambhava* mantra for more than an hour,

and then improvised a twenty-nine minute poem beginning with the line, 'How sweet to be born here in America' (Miles 439). Ginsberg would later expand on the immediacy of improvisation and his 'first thought best thought' approach to writing in an essay entitled 'Meditation and Poetics' (1988). Central to this article is Ginsberg's suggestion that the 'purification' or 'de-conditioning' offered to the mind

by meditative practice leads to a more direct way of seeing, without the intervening veil of preconceived ideas – a sudden insight or 'satori,

occasionally glimpsed as aesthetic experience' (96). Ginsberg compares Ezra Pound's claim that 'the natural object is always the adequate symbol' with Trungpa's statement that '[t]hings are symbols of themselves' (97), and continues by aligning Olson's advice that 'one perception must move

instanter on another' with the 'dharmic practice of letting go of thoughts and allowing fresh thoughts to arise, rather than hanging on to one exclusive image' (99). Meditation and poetry are thus, for Ginsberg, related means to avoid the conditioned mind: 'the life

of mediation and the life of art are both based on a similar conception of spontaneous mind' (99). While Ginsberg's insight is also applicable to Cage's

Zen-based indifference to teleology and goal-oriented aesthetic production in favour of the immediacy of experience, the two writers approach the unconditioned mind in very different manners. When Ginsberg implies that poetic consciousness can be purified through meditation, he echoes a thought which is not at all unsympathetic to Zen. However, the wildly ecstatic and emotionally-

charged poems of Ginsberg express personal subjectivity in a manner that is foreign to the de-personalized and disciplined austerity of Zen aesthetics. Not surprisingly, Ginsberg's work is far closer to the Tibetan 'crazy wisdom' tradition championed by Trungpa than it is to Zen. This tradition is associated with Buddhist adepts who attempted to undercut social norms through spontaneous, seemingly 'crazy'

practices such as refusing to wear clothes or exhibiting mad or eccentric behaviour. 'For Trungpa,' writes Tony Trigilio, 'practitioners in the crazy wisdom school seek to achieve a state of mind paradoxically both untamed and awakened' (21). In his 1981 poem 'Why I Meditate,' for example, Ginsberg writes: 'I sit because the Dadaists screamed on Mirror Street /

I sit because the Surrealists ate angry pillows / I sit because the Imagists breathed calmly

in Rutherford and Manhattan' (851). While the anaphora of these lines recalls the formal constraint of Ginsberg's 'Howl'

and serves to organize and unify the 'untamed' content of the poem, the expression of an individual consciousness remains at the forefront. This is a poem about meditation, perhaps composed in an

undisciplined, improvisatory, 'wildly' spontaneous manner, but it still dualistically represents a self who ruminates on the act of meditation. The poem is not a meditation – it is a meta-discourse, a text about meditation, and any insight remains filtered through the intentions and perceptions

of an individual consciousness. Cage on the other hand employs chance operations and rigorous aesthetic constraints to eliminate the expressivity of the conditioned mind. Discipline was paramount for Cage – he described his work in an interview with Daniel Charles as a 'discipline of the ego,' and argued that 'the ego without discipline is closed, it tends to close

in on its emotions. Discipline is what ruins all that closure. With it one can open up to the outside, as well as to the inside' (*For* 58). Discipline is thus for Cage the antithesis of emotional expression, which

he sees as being tied to the delusional ego and dualistically closed-off to the 'outer' or phenomenal world. Austere as it may appear, discipline breaks down the artificial barrier between outside and inside, self and other, because it limits the expression of a particular, seemingly individualized self. Moreover,

discipline can move the work into unexpected, entirely unplanned territory, free from the aesthetic likes and dislikes of the individual writer. There is in Cage no single, unified 'I' who speaks or reflects on a specific theme or complex of themes. ¶ It may be enlightening to further compare Cage's disciplined writing process with another of

his contemporaries, the poet and Zen monk Philip Whalen. Like Ginsberg, Whalen has most often been associated with the Beat movement. In the influential anthology *The New American Poetry* edited by Donald Allen in 1960, Whalen describes his

writing as 'a picture or graph of a mind moving, which

is a world body being here and now which is history [. . .] and you' (420). Notice that Whalen's statement defines the mind moving beyond individual consciousness, towards a 'world body' which collapses the distinction between the present and

history

as well as between the speaker and another 'you.' Whalen describes his poetry as the representation of a dynamic and transpersonal 'mind' which is not bound by space or time or by the distinction between subject and object. Jane Falk points out that Whalen's statement recalls the Zen practice of seated meditation, in which 'the practitioner sits silently, following the breath,

aware of the mind's movement' (105). From

this perspective the content of the poem is congruent to the content of the mind, recorded as Whalen observes it, and for Falk this practice recalls the Buddhist concept of *pratityasamutpada* – that is, the mutual conditioning or 'conditioned arising of all things (105). Whalen's method was relatively

straightforward: first he recorded his thoughts and observations in a notebook, where he was free to write spontaneously, without recourse to editing. He then gathered the 'best of what he had written' (Christensen 559) and spliced the notebook entries together, along with fragments of texts on Buddhist and Western literature, history, philosophy and religion. For example,

in the book-length serial poem *Every Day 1964–1965*, Whalen combines references to Buddhist scripture ('The

Lotus Sutra, Naturalized') with syntactically compressed phrasing ('I got drunk your house / You put that diamond my shirt pocket') and the use of ungrammatical American ideolects ('don't nobody know' [*Collected* 357]). Whalen's poem 'Composition' from the same collection begins with images of a speaker fidgeting with 'fingers ears and nose' and then 'putting

on hats in front of the mirror [. . .] mugging and posing' (*Collected* 366). As a metaphor for the compositional process, this

playfulness results in the 'smallest imaginable shimmy' creating a 'giant Bacchanal' (366), suggesting that for Whalen, composition is an act of light-hearted celebration, what he calls in the book's preface a 'continuous fabric (nerve movie?)' existing for a 'few hours of total attention and pleasure' (*Collected* 835). 'Composition' then

contrasts this lively freedom with the image of a piano as a 'closed system; / Even if you play on it with feathers, rocks, rubber tubing, /

Dear John Cage' (366). Here, Whalen refers to Cage's innovation of composing for a prepared piano. For

Tom Clark, these lines indicate how Whalen's poetic strategy of 'inspired puttering' continually returns to obsessive themes and rhythms, like the closed system of a tuned piano (1). ¶ While it is accurate to say that Whalen's work often returns to 'noodling or doodling as creative procedure' and that this procedure is 'characteristic of his disarmingly self-deflating comedy'

(Clark 1), it seems to me that this poem sets up a contrast between Whalen's good-humoured, open-ended poetics with a more closed-off system which is 'already there' and found in Cage – that is, a system which

exists before the 'nerve movie' or moment-by-moment process of the poem's composition. Cage was more concerned with setting up a disciplined, procedural constraint through the use of chance operations, and then letting that constraint run its course, than he was with charting the on-going process of his own phenomenological experience. However, Whalen light-heartedly offsets his critique by presenting it

in the form of a topsy-turvy letter to Cage, with the address line 'Dear John Cage' occurring at the end of the poem. Of course, this line could alternatively be read as a

term of endearment for Cage, as if he was a dear friend of Whalen – a possibility that further lightens the tone of the poem. Each of the serial poems in Whalen's

Every Day is dated and functions as a record of the poet's daily writing practice, and the resulting book 'graphs'

the discontinuities and changes of his awareness, and conveys the 'speed and multiphasic complexity of the alert mind' (Christensen 559). Whalen's compositional method thus provides a means to work 'outside the province of intentional composition' (Christensen 559). However, there remains in Whalen's work an intention to make choices about what to include in the poem, and this intention

is based on a value judgement about quality: what constitutes the 'best' bits of the notebooks? How does the writer distinguish what he likes from what he does not like, and does not want to include in the final poem? 'To set up what you like against what you dislike' writes the sixth-century *Chàn*

master Seng-t'san, 'is the disease of the mind' (1).[22] ¶ Contrast Whalen's graph of the mind moving with Cage's method for composing *Empty Words* (1974), one of his various revisions of Thoreau's *Journal*. After describing a complicated series of numerical equations based on the chance operations, Cage writes, '[k]nowing how many

pages there are in the *Journal*, one can then locate

[words, syllables and letters] by means of the *I Ching*' (*Empty* 11). Cage uses the *I Ching* to select bits of textual detritus from the *Journal*, and then employs the oracle again to reorganize his source material as non-intentional poetry: 'not l o the in in and that heSt and and / on all but the terminal leaves' (*Empty* 15). Unlike the strong remnant

of intentionality that remains in Whalen's writing, Cage employs chance operations to compose his work, thereby severely limiting personal judgements about quality. And unlike Whalen's use of his own journal as a source text from which to cobble together a new poem, Cage mines the *Journal* of someone else, thereby further removing his working process from personal subjectivity. As Cage himself writes, 'I use chance operations instead of operating according to my likes and dislikes. I use my work to change myself and I accept what the chance operations say' ('Taking' 11). ¶ In a letter to Allen Ginsberg written during the same

year that Whalen composed his note on poetry as a 'graph of the mind's movement,' Whalen described Zen as an attempt to 'eat that old, imaginary

self each one of us imagines we "have", in order to make way for the "real self"' (qtd. in Falk 104). This 'real self' is another way to describe

the Buddhist 'no self' or *anātman*, which is realized when one becomes aware of the empty and interconnected character of all phenomena. To perceive any single phenomenon as a unique and isolated

thing is for Buddhists a delusion which can be cured through recognizing the empty character of those objects. That realization paradoxically entails a psychological transformation in which the mind attains a state of 'no mind,' where the perception of objects, sounds, words, odours and so on is intensified beyond the unenlightened perceptions of conditioned consciousness. The ninth-century Zen master

THE IMITATION OF NATURE IN HER MANNER OF OPERATION   97

Kyōgen's experience of coming to enlightenment provides a good example of this heightened sense of awareness. Kyōgen was an erudite Buddhist scholar who underwent *kōan* study under the direction of Isan Reiyū, a master who gave him the *kōan*: 'what is your essential face before you were born?' Unable to solve this *kōan* through his reliance on scholarship and conceptual thought, Kyōgen burned his books in despair, and vowed to spend the rest of his life practicing meditation as a hermit. One day, while he was sweeping around his hermitage a pebble bounced off his broom and hit a bamboo tree. Hearing the sound, Kyōgen immediately experienced great enlightenment (Yamada 33). What is significant about this story is the fact that Kyōgen's *kenshō* occurred when his meditation practice transformed his sense perceptions. In fact, the literature of Zen repeatedly stresses how meditation allows one to experience sensations directly, without obstruction. Zen is conceived as a route towards 'pure reception' (Shute 293) and the practice of zazen leads to a situation of mental openness to encounters with phenomenon. Perhaps the same could be said of Whalen's poetry, because his 'graph' functions as a record of heightened mental awareness. Regardless of their compositional differences, both Whalen and Cage shared a desire to move towards a new form of Buddhist consciousness, which would take their readers beyond the limitations of pre-conditioned social identity.

Whalen creates an interface between 'what is going on inside the poet-speaker's mind and what is going on in the outside world' (Falk 117), thereby breaking down the dualistic boundary between self and other, and offering in its a place a representation of transpersonal experience. In contrast, for Cage, this new awareness occurs through simply listening with awareness, through the purposeful pursuit of purposelessness, through the disciplined employment of non-intentional compositional methods, and through a realization of 'nothing.' ¶ 'In Eckhart, the greatest Christian mystic, we find the same idea expressed in other terms: 'The Nothing is without beginning, therefore to make us in his own image, God created us out of Nothing.' Mark: *in his own image.* Was God then also Nothing?' (Beckett 20).To illustrate

Cage's engagement with the negated image – the nothing of Zen – it is useful to

visit his interest in the fourteenth-century Christian Mystic Meister Eckhart. In 1970,Cage placed the early, 'two-volume translation' of Eckhart on his list of all-time top ten books, explaining that Eckhart's work echoed the non-dualism of Zen: 'West is East: No separation' ('List' 139). Suzuki was also drawn to Eckhart due to the mystic's depiction of God's creation coming out of timelessness, nothingness,

and 'Absolute Void,' a depiction which Suzuki understood

as being analogous to Buddhist *śūnyatā* (*Mysticism* 6). Cage's Buddhist leanings mean that

he seldom mentions God, and with few

exceptions, his brief references to the Judeo-Christian tradition take the form of short anecdotes about Eckhart and his teachings

or else direct quotations drawn directly from the mystic's writing: 'Dear God, I beg

you to rid me of God' (*Silence* 193). This prayer illustrates Eckhart's desire to be free of spiritual preconceptions, so that he might attain an awareness of the divine based on his own experience rather than on the mediated images of his social context. Cage's desire for 'silence' echoes this sentiment without using such terms as 'God'

or 'Soul' or 'Spirit.' And much like Cage's 'nothing,' Eckhart frequently resorts to negation in order to speak about the divine. In

his sermon on 'Works Inward and Outward,' Eckhart writes of withdrawing into a 'state of mind free from all images and definition, and without any activity at all, subjective or objective' (26). Eckhart could thus be considered as an exponent of apophatic or 'negative' theology, a discourse in which knowledge of the divine is achieved through successive denials of the divine. Kevin Hart argues

that the negative theologian

places theological language 'under erasure' (203), meaning that s/he uses the language of theology against itself: the positive theologian makes claims about what God is, while the negative theologian uses the positive theologian's vocabulary to describe what God is not. Eckhart cites the writings of the sixth-century Christian philosopher Pseudo-Dionysius to

exemplify this view: 'how can one work with God? By being dead to self and to all activities. St. Dionysius says, "He speaks best of God who in the fullness of his interior riches can best hold his peace"' (37). Hart similarly quotes Pseudo-Dionysius to exemplify the silencing of theological language, the apophatic

situation of language

about the divine under erasure: 'nor is It personal essence, or eternity, or time; nor can It be grasped by the understanding, since It is not knowledge or truth; nor is It kingship or wisdom; nor is It a one, nor is It unity [. . .]' (qtd. in Hart 176). Pseudo-Dionysius negates terms traditionally applied to God by positive theologians in

order to state what God is not. The form of his discourse deconstructs the idea that the deity exists as a positive term, such as the Archimedean point of the Greco-Christian *Logos*. This strategy is similarly followed by Cage, whose turn towards indeterminacy, non-sense and silence in the context of Buddhism negates any positive explanation or rational conception about 'reality,' while simultaneously presenting readers with a site for direct, non-conceptual experience. However, in Cage's Buddhist example there is no deity, so

his negations are not to be taken as a form of theology,

but as

a form of Buddhist ontology. Nevertheless, Cage's 1992 mesostic lecture 'Overpopulation and Art' shows a degree of inter-faith dialogue[23] by including further references to the Christian tradition, as well as to the so-called 'suchness' of Buddhism ('every being / including

the telephone / is the bUddha' [15]):

> [. . .] reviVing
> practicE
> of chRistianity
> sPlit the stick
> O
> sPlit the stick and there is
> jesUs
> waLking
> on the wAlking
> on The
> wrItng
> O
> oN
> the wAter [. . .] (22).

In this brief excerpt, Cage points to the notion of 'reviving' the practice of Christianity through mystical awareness. He cites the non-canonical *Gospel of Thomas*, where Jesus is represented as saying 'split a piece of wood, and I am there' (Lambdin 77) as well as the Biblical account of Jesus walking on water.

'Overpopulation and Art' was delivered at Stanford University a few months before Cage's death in 1992,

and it serves to sum up his later work's concern with political and social realities, as well as his call for the necessity of finding 'nEw / foRms of living

together' (23) through what he saw as the related pursuits of avant-garde art-making practice, non-violent anarchism,

Buddhist awareness, and the revival of esoteric Western spirituality. ¶ Cage's 'Composition as Process' (1958) cites Suzuki's teachings on interpenetration, a term which Cage uses to describe all phenomena as 'MOVING OUT IN ALL DIRECTIONS / PENETRATING AND BEING PENETRATED BY

EVERY OTHER ONE NO MATTER / WHAT THE TIME OR

WHAT THE SPACE' (*Silence* 46). Cage employs the term interpenetration to indicate his belief that each and every thing in time and space is related to each and every other thing. While it is true to say that the central Buddhist tenet of dependent origination suggests that objects have a conditioned past, a present, and a

future, this is not the whole story. What was once a soft-wood tree, for example, has become in the present tense the space 'printed' on this page, which will eventually decompose before combining with other objects to become something new, equally

marked by impermanence. To the conditioned mind, objects appear to have a material history

which can be isolated,

conceptualized, and described. The result may provide some understanding of the object, and yet, without the Zen no mind experience of the non-conditioned, that understanding is incomplete. For at

each stage of the page's history, there is no time when the page is fully and only

a page; one could say that what we call a page is overdetermined by numerous other karmic factors, all of

which contribute to the seeming existence of the phenomenon we label as a page as well as the phenomena we label as past, present and future. This is precisely where the concept of interpenetration is most easily recognizable: time itself, like the objects which seem to exist in time, is entirely empty of intrinsic essence, because *śūnyatā* is timeless. The paradox is that

while things do exist, they exist in time, and yet both time and those things are empty of existence. Perhaps Dōgen's words in the *Shōbōgenzō* may shed some light on the concept of interpenetration: '[t]he way the self arrays itself is the form of the entire world. See each thing in this entire world as a moment of time' (76–77). Deane Curtin points out that here Dōgen sees Buddha-nature as 'completely actual in each moment' (199), and that for Dōgen any encounter with the 'true self' of this actuality is phenomenological, to the extent that it must be experienced as 'multiple, as interpenetrating other beings' (200). For Cage, the interpenetration of space and time means that there is no need to proceed in such dualistic terms as

success and failure, the beautiful and the ugly, or good

and evil. Instead Cage relies on the spontaneous acceptance of results, without resorting to critical judgement: 'ALL YOU CAN DO IS SUDDENLY LISTEN / IN

THE SAME WAY THAT WHEN YOU CATCH COLD ALL / YOU CAN DO IS SUDDENLY SNEEZE' (*Silence* 46) ¶ To some extent Cage's

writing on the interpenetration of space and time resonate with the American poet Leslie Scalapino's work on temporality. Although Scalapino's work has most often been read and situated in the context of Language Writing, she traces much of her thinking about writing and representation to her early immersion in Asian culture and philosophy and to alternative, non-Western ideological beliefs (Frost 319; Tan 195). Scalapino is concerned with 'the sense that

phenomena unfold. (What is it or) how is it that the viewer sees the impression of history created, created by oneself though its occurring outside?' (*How* 119). Much of Scalapino's writing attends to how perception

creates historical narrative, as well as to how language might enact the immediate moment (Frost 319). Kathy Ann Tan observes that Scalapino's

'writing about an event in the past is in itself a new event, one that takes place in "new time"' (212). For instance, in the serial poem *New Time* (1999), which Tan describes accurately as a syntactically disjunctive and linguistically challenging work (212), Scalapino writes: 'to see what you had, chronologically, otherwise one was transgressing it – now it is "transgressing"

it' (35). The point here and elsewhere in *New Time* does

not seem to be about a specific transgression, but to be about the self-reflexive collapsing of chronology into a kind of Steinian continuous present, in order to bring readers into the present moment, the 'now' of the poem as it is read. The events represented in Scalapino's poetry may be based on events occurring in

real time, such as in the segment: 'rain: falling in sheets at the time. Sitting floating (not in

it) (fictive there while occurring)' (3). However, this rain is now fictive, because I and/or you read this passage and think of a rain fall that is absent, yet still 'occurring' or present in a moment of mental representation, which is the 'new time' of the event of rain. As

Jason Lagapa points out, Scalapino's writing radically re-assesses the act of observation, particularly as observation 'can be understood as the ontological grounding of

an individual subject' (38). *New Time*'s breakdown of the distinction between reader and writer and between past and present offers us a means to question subjectivity: if the event represented in the text is observed by a reader at the present moment of the reading, at what point

does the writer's subjective

experience become the reader's subjective experience? Scalapino notes that segments in her 1985 poem *that they were at the beach— aeolotropic writing* are the 'actual act or event itself – occurring

long after it occurred; or acts put into it which occurred more recently' (*How* 21). Scalapino's disintegration of the borders between

past, present and future is characteristic of much of her poetry, and her critical writing makes it evident that her interest in collapsing temporal distinctions owes something to her study of Zen Buddhism. In 'Language as Transient Act' (2007), for example, Scalapino writes

that Philip Whalen 'frequently created a compression of all times onto one in a poem' so that the present is 'only empty there (has no nature in itself, is words)' with the future and past being a series of 'presents-without-entity [which] appear to rise from each other' (xxxvi). Scalapino compares Whalen's superimposition of time

to 'Dōgen's articulation of being as time' – that is, the interpenetration of time, in which

'past, future, and present are going on separately and not excluding each other' (xxxvi). In more conventional terms, writing is by its very nature chronological: simply put, one word follows another. And yet, Scalapino's Zen-based poetry and critical writing re-orient the reader's perception of chronology by foregrounding a non-dualistic experience of past and present. One could say that Scalapino's work addresses the future by dissolving the boundary between past history and present experience. ¶ Cage pursues a very different approach regarding

the interpenetration of time. His poem-lecture 'Where Are We Going? And What Are We Doing?' (1961) documents a 'simultaneous performance' of four distinct voices occurring in real time. Cage does not superimpose the

actual texts on the page, but uses the page instead to indicate the texts which he intends to be heard as four simultaneous lectures. Once again, his entropological attention to the materiality of writing stems from a desire to overturn the limitations of the

unified self in relation to nature; Cage writes that we are not in the 'driver's seat' with respect to nature, and he suggests that while the

texts in this lecture function like life and

nature in their meaninglessness, the 'grand thing about the human mind is that it can turn its own tables and see meaninglessness as ultimate meaning' (*Silence* 195). The layout of 'Where Are We Going? And What Are We Doing?' employs bold fonts and italics to distinguish between

THE IMITATION OF NATURE IN HER MANNER OF OPERATION 111

the different voices of the simultaneous performance. While the resulting lecture is highly disjunctive because of its continual interruptions – its stops and starts in time – this form of documenting the performance does not faithfully reproduce the way that a listener would experience the piece. To a certain degree, this choice of layout domesticates the piece by removing its sonic qualities, which

hinge on the mutual cancellation of communicable words. True, there are large sections of this lecture which include one, two or three voices instead of the full four, and these sections are indicated by full stops

and white space in the place of the absent voice:

If we set out to catalogue things
.

.

. (*Silence* 195).

Given Cage's view that 'silence' is not the same as the complete absence of sound, it is possible that the blank pages in the text function as sites for ambient acoustic information, thereby generating further indeterminate relations between sound and silence. And although Cage introduces his 'Where Are We Going? And What Are We Doing' lecture by claiming

it is based on his understanding of

the way that nature operates, the text departs from the tradition of

nature writing from the outset, because instead of referencing an object in the natural world or a topological scene,

it self-consciously foregrounds language itself as a natural phenomenon. By superimposing voices in a cacophony of linguistic excess, Cage complicates any straightforward reading or understanding, thereby calling

into question the transparent norms of communication so typical of nature writing, and offering instead information as non-sense. Mac Low recalls attending a performance of this lecture at the Pratt Institute in 1961. 'Empty lines indicate[d] silence,' he comments,

and much of the lecture was unintelligible because of the simultaneity of the performer's voices (215). Mac Low further points out that the communicative function of the English language was for Cage, detrimental to poetry. By limiting

language to communication we have, in Cage's words, 'nearly destroyed the potential for poetry' (*Silence* 224; qtd. in Mac Low 215).

Cage's inscriptions of linguistic non-information further function as spatialized nodes of empty noise, where paradoxically, nothing is communicated but silence.

NOT JUST SELF- BUT SOCIAL REALIZATION

Although Cage was never psychoanalysed beyond an initial consultation,[1] his Zen teacher D. T. Suzuki was extremely sympathetic to various schools of psychoanalysis. Suzuki participated with Erich Fromm and other prominent neo-Freudians at a 1957 workshop on 'Zen Buddhism and Psychoanalysis' in

Mexico, and C. G. Jung wrote the foreword to the German edition of Suzuki's *Introduction to Zen Buddhism* (1948). In *Living by Zen* (1950) Suzuki describes śūnyatā as 'inert and contentless' (60) and as the emptiness of the 'cosmic Unconscious' (88). Presumably Suzuki has in mind here the unconsciousness of the 'big mind' of Zen, rather than the

mind of the individual ego; as Eric Mortenson writes, 'the road to "big mind" leads through the notion of emptiness' (128). Or as Cage's friend and former student the poet Jackson Mac Low suggests, the term 'unconscious' used by Suzuki and other writers on Zen should

be taken as a synonym for the 'no-mind' of enlightenment, 'which is not individual but universal' (226). Cage, on the other hand, remained sceptical about psychoanalysis in any form. In an after note to 'Lecture on Nothing,' he relates the story of a preliminary consultation he had with an analyst. When the analyst advised him

that treatment would enable him to write much more music, Cage replied 'Good heavens! I already write too much' (*Silence* 127) and he was put off by analysis altogether. What strikes me as

significant about this story is the way the analyst assumes that an individual's capacity to labour is a sign for mental health. Here the psychoanalyst (perhaps unconsciously) upholds the economic value

of maximum production and the related ideology which casts the individual in the role of happy producer. The analyst also presents himself as a subject who knows, and who is able to interpret and potentially master the problem of the analysis. Perhaps if Cage had met a Lacanian analyst he would have felt differently about undergoing a course of analysis, because

Lacan criticized American psychoanalysis during the 1950s for attempting to cover over the duality of the one who suffers and the one who heals, with the opposition between the

one who knows and the one who does not. The American context cast the analyst in the role of 'the good, strong parent, the ultimate role

model, without ever questioning the imaginary structuring of that role, nor how it minoritized the patient and enhanced the analyst's self-deluded prestige' (Gallop 29). ¶ Lacanian psychoanalysis takes

a different tack. For one thing, Lacan's theories include the recognition of a 'register' of experience that is beyond the capacity of language to describe or enunciate. The Lacanian Real is a field of non-knowledge which cannot be conceptualized or described, a 'plenum without fissures, divisions, oppositions, or differentiations' (Moncayo 344). The Real is 'impossible to imagine, impossible to integrate into the symbolic order,

and impossible to attain in any way' (Evans 160). Cage's Zen-inspired work invites us to experience the unconscious that *cannot* be known, for his writing

continually provides a non-discursive yet compelling experience of nothing. Self, language, natural phenomenon, stuff: all

empty, all taking part in non-dualistic interdependence, all unconscious, and all traversed by the Real. ¶ Perhaps more striking for psychoanalysis is Cage's representation of a 'time-life' or 'chrono biological' body, materialized through the use of empty space on the page. For Michael Holquist, the body is both temporal and textual: 'body clocks organize the activities of cells, tissues, and hormones in a way that uses time to provide internal information about external conditions: the body, in other words, is dialogic' (25). If the body is a dialogic sign system or language, it is potentially

translatable. In effect, the spatial notation found in Cage

can be read as a type of 'intersemiotic translation,' (a term coined by Roman Jakobson in 1959 as a means to interpret linguistic signs by non-linguistic sign systems, such as the ekphrastic translation of verbal language into painted image).

By foregrounding the body as text, Cage presents the page as

a site for the mutual interdependence of somatic ('natural') and symbolic ('cultural') registers. However, the intersemiotic translation of body events does not necessarily imply the presence of a universal, ahistorical, and acultural body language; the body is a sign

system which cannot exist apart from social and linguistic phenomena. Cage's implication of the body in language invites readers to apprehend the relation between word and non-word, somatic 'language' and the symbolic order, nature and culture.

The empty space represented by Cage's 'nothing'

functions as a kind of non-site for the body – that is, for the immediate experience of a living, breathing body as it is translated through time and language. ¶ This form of spatialized, 'chronobiological' body shares some affinities with Lacan's late

investigations into language and power, at least to the extent that both the time-life body and Lacan call into question established modes of enunciating knowledge. In his *Seminar XVII* of 1971,

Lacan posits four discourses which organize social relations: the master, the university, the hysteric, and the analyst. These discourses are not specifically

inhabited by individuals, but are relational. Put another way, these discourses are 'four possible articulations of the networks regulating intersubjective relations' (Žižek *Looking* 130). The discourse of the master holds a privileged place among the four discourses; it provides a 'master signifier,' which must be obeyed, and which consequently occupies a position of power. As Bruce Fink writes of the master

signifier, 'no justification is given for his or her power – it just is' (31). The master signifier is also unconcerned about knowledge. The problem for the master signifier is that there is some disturbing surplus, some lack which escapes its power, an object which, in Lacan's terms, 'presents itself as the most opaque in

the effects of discourse' (*Other* 43). We could say that the time-life body in Cage stands in for this missing remnant, which cannot be symbolized by the master discourse. ¶ In the discourse of the university, systematic knowledge is the

ultimate authority. In order to present knowledge, the discourse of the university must repress the time-life body – in effect, the discourse of the university represses the surplus remnant of bodily experience which escapes power. There is a hegemonic relationship between the discourses of the master and the university, because the power

of the master signifier lurks behind what seems to be neutral, unbiased knowledge. As Lacan writes, 'for centuries, knowledge has been pursued as a defence against truth' (qtd. in Fink 33). The discourse of the university is key to interpellation, to the subject's assumption of a socially acceptable position within the symbolic order. However, since there

is always a surplus remnant which escapes symbolization (in

this case, the blank space as a site for the intersemiotic translation of the time-life body), the discourse of the university's act of repression leads to lack. For Lacan, one of the key misrecognitions propounded by the discourse of the university (in alliance with the master's power) is the notion that the subject takes the phenomenon of consciousness as

unified and autonomous. One key element of the discourse of the university is its failure to unveil this misrecognition; instead of questioning the master's discourse, it supports power by constructing the 'subject who knows,' who misrecognizes him or her self as a complete and autonomous individual. Lacan coins the neologism 'I-cracy' to illustrate this complex: 'from every academic statement by any

philosophy whatsoever [. . .] the *I-cracy* emerges, irreducibly' (*Other* 63). ¶ The discourse of the hysteric begins to move beyond the hegemonic relationship upheld by the master/university complex of discourses. Hysterical discourse articulates the expression of

a fissure; on the one hand, this discourse recognizes the existence of a subject position, situated in the symbolic order or social network (e.g. 'I am a worker, a teacher, an employee, an artist, a student, etc.'). On the other hand, this discourse also questions the non-

symbolized surplus of unrealizable desire or lack which has been produced by the symbolic. In effect, the

hysteric discourse embodies this gap, this 'question of being' (Žižek *Looking* 131). While the university discourse acts in alliance with the master discourse, the hysteric

challenges the master by pushing the limits of knowledge into uncertainty, thereby maintaining the contradiction between conscious knowledge and unconscious desire. The hysteric does not gloss over this split by trying to make phenomena fit into an ordered and

containable whole. The time-life body passes through the discourse of the hysteric because it contrasts conscious and rational language with the unconscious and indeterminate surplus of bodily excess. This body in language is hysterical in the sense of Žižek's politicized recasting of the term 'hysteria' – that is, as an indication of the subject's resistance to interpellation: 'what is the hysterical question if not an articulation of the incapacity of the subject to fulfil the symbolic identification, to assume fully and without restraint the symbolic mandate?' (*Sublime* 113). The time-life

body exhibits hysterical symptoms by blocking the subject's desire for conceptual knowledge. Instead of following a desire for the university discourse's promise of knowledge as satisfaction, the time-life body desires dissatisfaction through indeterminacy and through the textual embodiment of physical, lived experience. Cage's experiential 'nothing' desires to have its desire for meaning impeded, in order to frustrate symbolic totalization. To situate Cage's time-life

body in the discourse of the hysteric is to illustrate how it articulates the

experience of a fissure between the signifier that represents a socially established practice of knowledge, and the non-symbolized, affective surplus that is repressed by the symbolic order. ¶ The split subjectivity that is found in the discourse of the hysteric does not mean that the unconscious is accessible (and therefore manageable) to the hysteric; Lacan saw the hysteric's discourse as an essential step in a process that culminates in the discourse of the analyst. This final discourse is somewhat

paradoxical, because

it attempts to speak from the position of the element that escapes

speech. In the context of Cage's spatialized writing practice, we could say that the discourse of the analyst stems from the time-life body, which in turn is derived from the 'nothing' of Zen. The body materialized by Cage as a 'nothing' discursifies what

has been repressed by the master/university hegemony of discourses.

Here the subject begins to experience a transformation

in its relationship to the symbolic order. In effect, the discourse of the analyst produces a new master signifier for the subject, and in Cage, this new signifier

is *silence*. For Lacan, real social change will only occur once the subject can produce this new, un-totalizing and adaptable master signifier. ¶ The unique perspective that Lacan's four discourses offer allows us to consider the potential for the time-life body to effect social change, because the

time-life body provides an exemplary site for undermining the discourse of the master. Cage's 'nothing' points to an alternative mode of representing subjectivity – one that takes the body and lived experience into account, at a material level. In contrast to the 'living book' of his performative writing, the ordinary or dead book

is closer to the discourse of the university, due to its stress on the transmission of clear and distinct knowledge, presented in terms aimed at

a universal body of educated subjects who practise that knowledge – a form of discourse that Lacan would call 'the fantasy of a totality-knowledge' (*Other* 33). In effect, the time-life body as a space for

silence or 'nothing' foregrounds the complex relationships formed among knowledge, language, the body, materiality and subjectivity. This arena of investigation complicates any straightforward reading, thereby calling into question the university discourse's fantasy of rationally communicated meaning. Cage's time-life texts function as sites for the eruption of non-sense – a seemingly pejorative term which would ordinarily be repressed by the discourse of the university in its

attempt to seamlessly produce knowledge. Instead of setting up language as something to

be interpreted, the time-life body reframes its referent by foregrounding that referent as a textual construction – that is, as a translation of body into language and silence, organized as 'poetry.' This dismantling of knowledge-production further entails a dismantling of the individual, self-present subject. The 'I' of Cage's time-life body is

not the unified subject or individual as hero of liberating knowledge found in the university discourse. It is instead a textual 'I' which destabilizes the unicity of conventional reading and its construction of the classical subject of knowledge, the subject who can answer with his name or with the word

'I' to the question 'who is speaking?' The time-life body could thus be recast in Lacanian terms as 'I am that which I am not,' or in Žižek's reformulation: 'I am conscious of myself only insofar as I am out of reach to myself' (*Tarrying* 15).

Following this logic, the time-life body entirely dismisses the idea of finding a 'voice' in favour of producing the phrase without subject and of saying 'nothing.' ¶ As nature writing, texts such as *Mureau* or *Empty Words* do not lament the loss of our natural environment. Nor do they return to the ancient myth of Gaia, the living planetary ecosphere where humans, animals, plants and the Earth mother all live together in harmony. Cage's foregrounding of a subjective void in the face of nature, rather than an organic, holistic paradigm which subsumes culture into nature, is not entirely unlike Žižek's writing on the environmental crisis. True, this crisis has intensified a cultural desire to shift from the mechanistic, anthropocentric paradigm, in which humans manipulated nature as an object of technological domination, to a new paradigm which 'conceives of nature as a living organism' (Žižek *On* 185). But for Žižek, the ecological belief in the interdependence of humans and the earth occurs precisely because we are unwilling to 'confront the abyss of the subject' (186), and because we repress that subjective void by finding self-identity in a symbolic network which enables us to 'experience the universe as a meaningful totality'

(186). The predominant ecological ideology

interpellates subjects into the assumption of determinate social positions *vis à vis* a belief in an

ordered cosmos: 'in this way, the chaos of the encounter of the real is transformed into a meaningful narrative' (186). While it may appear that Cage's Zen-based nature poetics fall into this narrative, his texts say no to interpellation

by refusing to cohere at a thematic level. Instead, Cage presents a radical subject as void, with nothing to say, in an encounter with the Real of nature in all its senselessness.

Here Cage presents us with a paradox that resembles the indeterminacy of traditional *kōan* literature. On the one hand, Cage's various references to Buddhism, to ecology and Thoreau, and to finding new, holistic 'foRms of

living together' ('Overpopulation' 23) seem to present us with the type of 'meaningful narrative' which Žižek finds so problematic, and which he argues is central to interpellation. Žižek's critique could be applied to Cage when his texts present the *idea* of wholeness in a discursive, conceptual form and from this perspective Cage's writing could be situated in the Lacanian discourse of the university, with its systematic and rationally-grounded presentation of knowledge. On the other hand, however, the performative aspect of Cage's writing provides us with a space for non-conceptual experience – for a reading that is not bound by semantics, but which is available to be lived through by the time-life

body.

Cage's spatial practice does not uphold the old, unified Cartesian self or its related neoliberal version which sees the self as an independent entity, free to dominate nature for commercial gain. Nor do his performative texts represent the theme of Buddhist subjectivity at the level of content, preferring instead to use radical experimentation with literary form to

signify Buddhist interdependence. The resulting contradiction

between performative

experience and conceptual knowledge bypasses the hail of the discourse of the university. ¶ We could say that the blank spaces occupying many of Cage's texts bear

a structural resemblance

to Žižek's description of a journalistic photograph of the 1989 demonstrations in Bucharest, in which anti-

government rebels are shown celebrating the overthrow of Ceauşescu by ripping the red star from the centre of the Romanian flag. In Žižek's account, this hole represented a point of mobilization, the figure of a space 'not yet hegemonized by any positive ideological project' (*Tarrying* 1). Blank spaces or holes in Cage's text reflexively notate something which cannot be reconstituted as meaning –

they offer us a materialist performance of nature as the non-discursive space of experience. Yet what is perhaps more significant about Cage's nature writing *vis à vis* political struggle is that it points out the empty quality not only of language and subjectivity, but also of the void which ultimately informs hegemonic power. Cage's work exists in a paradoxically political yes and no: on the one hand, it functions in tandem with the dominant culture due to its firm entrenchment in the cultural spaces and practises which legitimate avant-garde practice, such as the concert hall, the state-funded museum or the prominent university press. As Henri Lefebvre writes on the ideology of these forms of contemporary art discourses: 'when there is talk

of art and culture, the real subject is money, the market, exchange, power' (389). From

this angle, Cage presents us with a form of spatial practice which interacts with the flows, transfers and interactions of capital. On the other hand – for those who have ears to hear – the experience of consuming Cage could be nuanced to illustrate a micro-political challenge

to institutional power; in terms of Lefebvre's so-called

representational space – that is, space as directly lived through its associated images and symbols (39), Cage offers us a representation of 'nothing' as a sign which can be experienced and perceived materially, but which is always left unconceptualized at the level of meaning. True, there is a message 'about' the void and nature in Cage's spatial practice, but space here cannot be reduced to a paraphrased statement or abstract conceptualization of that message. ¶ The critical reception of Cage's 'nothing' has often charged it with being socially irresponsible and apolitical in its outlook. As early as 1962, for example, Michael Steinberg argued that Cage is 'totally without social commitment' and that his compositions are of

historical

importance because they represent 'the complete abdication of the artist's power' (158). Similarly, Douglas Kahn's *Noise, Water, Meat: A History of Sound in the Arts* (1999) claims that 'one of the central effects of Cage's battery of silencing

techniques was a silencing of the social' (165). However, more recent Cage criticism has considered the complex relationship between Cage's work, silence and power in a different light. Ina Bloom points out that Kahn took issue with Cage's essentialist relegation of sound to the apolitical realm of

nature, and therefore Kahn regarded Cage's work as an attempt to deny 'participation in the kind of semiotic processes that pertain to social beings' (Bloom 172). In contrast to Kahn, Bloom argues that 'semiotics is no longer the dominant critical framework for the interpretation of the

relation between art and power, and Cage's naturalism, his emphasis on the

quasi-autonomous *life* of sounds, should be given a different place in a social landscape' (172). Bloom draws on the Foucauldian notion of biopolitics, in which power is 'enacted in an immanent field of complex interactivity' (172). One key element in his account is Cage's use of technology, especially in his

manipulation of magnetic tape to discover previously unheard dimensions of sound. Bloom suggests that the apprehension of these new sounds 'exposes you to infinite layers of complexity, to force fields that will affect you in uncharted ways' (173). And it is precisely this infinite complexity and 'force field' of

Cage's cultural production which models the complicated dynamics of modern power. If Cage's work 'once seemed to elude all questions of power,' writes Bloom, 'it was only because power itself was inadequately understood in terms of

hierarchical structures' (173). ¶ How do Cage's Zen plenitude of 'nothing' and his entropological, illegible poetics engage with the dynamics of contemporary power?

Aimé Patris once asked the French philosopher Georges Bataille if he was a Buddhist because of the Buddhist view that the concept of the person is illusory. Bataille responded by claiming that he felt closer to Buddhism than he did to Catholicism, although he did take issue with

the Buddhist recognition of transcendence (Bataille *Absence* 84). Nevertheless, Bataille's writing on religion, the sacred, and writing may shed some light (or darkness) on Cage's nothing in relation to power. Following Emile Durkheim's characterization of the

'sacred' as anything that is absolutely other to the profane, Bataille argues that the sacred consists of everything that is rejected by society as either refuse or as superior transcendent value. Bataille's version of the sacred is not to be understood as support

for faith in a deity or some form of religious ideology, but with the implication of incommensurate otherness. This otherness includes literature; as Martin Jay has argued, Bataille upheld obscurity in writing because it challenges lucid prose as a 'clear passage of

ideas from one subjectivity to another' (Jay 230). Cage's texts could thus be read as forms of 'sovereign communication' – that is, communication that can only occur when 'we resort to evil, that is to say the

violation of the law' (Bataille *Literature* 172). As a sacred and transgressive discourse, Cage's writing expends meaning and challenges the transmission of knowledge as a support for the self-conscious subject. Steve McCaffery argues that this form of literary expenditure is 'entirely devoid of self-interest' and is directed towards 'break-down and discharge rather than accumulation and integration' (213).Cage's Zen 'nothing' is

politically akin to what McCaffery has called a 'politics beyond politics' (153), because Cage's empty words agitate the standard grammatical and nominal formats in which

knowledge is transmitted. Cage's texts are sacred in Bataille's sense of the term because their illegibility violates socially normative laws of communication.[2] In relation to consumer-oriented cultural production or to mainstream literature, they appear as territories or spaces of otherness. Perhaps Cage's texts are also sacred in the sense given to the word by Zen – that is, they are *not* sacred. When the Indian monk and first *Ch'an* patriarch Bodhidharma introduced Buddhism to China, Emperor Wu asked him: 'What is the highest truth of the holy doctrine?' Bodhidharma answered the Emperor with a spatial metaphor: 'boundless expanse and *nothing* that can be called holy' (emphasis added; Kapleau 257). Christmas Humphreys provides a gloss: 'in the Void there are

no distinctions. Nothing is more or less sacred

than anything else. Here one thinks the thought of Non-Thought.' (204). If there is no opposition between the sacred and the profane, and no phenomenon is more or less sacred than any other phenomenon, how does one justify making choices about anything? Žižek's writing on free choice may be relevant; Žižek argues that contemporary capitalism makes capitulation to an imposed option

appear to subjects as free choice. For Žižek, the subject has two types of freedom: on the one hand, there is 'formal freedom,' which is 'the freedom of choice WITHIN the coordinates of existing power

relations,' while on the other hand, there is 'actual freedom,' which is the 'site of an intervention which undermines these very coordinates' (*On* 122). And while Žižek is hostile to Western Buddhism because he sees it as escapist (*On* 12), Cage's entropological iteration of a subject as void calls into question the supposed freedom of choice which

is still offered to all Americans as individuals. Žižek suggests that Western Buddhism offers subjects a means to 'drift along, while retaining an inner

distance and indifference' in the face of the unsettling pace of technological and social change (*On* 13). What his critique misses is the fact that Buddhism regards the notion of a unique and personal identity as delusion – not only in theory, but as lived experience. Unlike the capitalist subject who believes he or she is free to choose, the empty subject of Zen Buddhism does not make free choices; in

Zen (and Cage) there is nothing to choose, and no one to choose it. ¶ From mid-1960s onwards Cage began to extend his Buddhist concern with the void and with non-intention into the social sphere. In *A Year From Monday: New Lectures and Writings* (1967), he

writes that his thought 'is and isn't changing' and that he is 'now concerned with improving the world' (ix). Cage argues that 'the disciplines, gradual and sudden (principally Oriental), formerly practiced by individuals to pacify their minds, bringing them into accord with ultimate reality – must now be practiced socially' (ix). The gradual approach mentioned by Cage refers to spiritual practices spanning long periods of time, in which the aspirant experiences an on-going expansion of compassion and detachment from the world. In the so-called

'sudden school,' on the other hand, enlightenment can come at any time, and in a flash or *kenshō* of insight.[3] Crucially, Cage ties his emerging concern with social issues to his experience and knowledge of Asian spiritual practice. 'Diary: How

to Improve the World (You Will Only Make Matters Worse) 1965' is his first overtly political text. Explicit political references in Cage before this time are infrequent,

and tend to be more whimsical than analytic or critical. 'Would you like to join / a society called / Capitalists Inc.,' Cage asks in *Silence*, '(Just so no one would / think we were / Communists)' (125). Here the text

seems to voice a fear that was shared by many intellectuals and artists living through the McCarthy era, who had to keep silent about their politically subversive beliefs and activities rather than suffer the consequences of social ostracism, loss of work, and the potential of being criminally charged. While Cage may ironically refer to such covert operations, when considered in the light of the very real political struggles occurring during the height of the cold war,

the tone of his question seems oddly irrelevant. Moreover, the us / them binary set up by the quotation appears on the surface to be alien to Cage's faith in Zen doctrine, which maintains that distinctions are illusory. As

the sixth-century *Ch'an* poem 'Verses on the Faith of Mind' affirms, '[a]s long as you tarry in the dualism, / How can

you realize Oneness?' (1). From this perspective, the ironic tone of the binary set up by Cage suggests that he is merely playing with political identities, and that he has no real interest in upholding either Capitalist ideology or Communist revolution. In any case, the later 'Diary' of 1965 employs chance operations to create what Cage called a

'mosaic of ideas, statements, words, and stories' (*Year* 3), and it advises readers to '[d]evelop / panopticity of mind'

(13) while describing daily life as 'disorganized, characterized by chaos, / illuminated anarchically' (16). The text's

recommendation to develop a panoptic or all-seeing mind is

reminiscent of the 'Big Mind' cultivated in Zen practice – that is,

an experience which is neither localized to

a single perspective nor limited to a unitary subject position or ego. However, the text also juxtaposes passages emphasizing Zen awareness

with a

newer, more cynical understanding of social and environmental conditions. For instance, Cage lists serious ecological problems such as the pollution of air and water, the extinction of animal species, and the elimination of forests, and then the ironic question: 'What would you call it? / Nirvana?' (18). ¶ As George J. Leonard has shown, earlier

Cage is based on the premise that there is no need for us to change the world, but simply to 'wake up to the life we are living, which is so excellent' (qtd. in Leonard 178). From the mid-1960s on, however, Cage augments his earlier quietism with a desire for social improvement through a highly

idiosyncratic version of Taoist and Buddhist anarchism. On the one hand, his call to change the world exemplifies an 'activist, how-to, can-do spirit' (Leonard 181).

Yet on the other hand, Cage concludes his title with a phrase sourced from the fourth-century BC Taoist philosopher and poet Chuang-tse ('you will only make matters worse'), thereby contradicting the activist spirit of the title's opening line. Leonard argues convincingly

that Cage's later work balances these two seemingly oppositional poles, and quotes the *Tao- te-Ching* as a summary of Cage's mature concerns: '[h]old fast enough to the silence / and of the ten thousand things all can be worked on by you' (185).

Much like the Zen experience of the emptiness of everyday things – the *suchness* of common place things – Cage's

citation

to Chuang-tse sets up a link between silence and the myriad objects of the real world. And in the light of Cage's study of Asian religious traditions, it is important to remember that anarchism is only a relatively recent Western phenomenon. For Peter Marshall, the

ancient sages of Taoism provide us with the first 'clear expression of an anarchist sensibility,' and the *Tao*

te Ching 'may be considered one of the greatest anarchist classics' (54). Marshall represents Taoism as a precursor to modern anarchism because of its rejection of all forms of imposed authority, government and private property in favour of a free society in which individuals would be left to themselves (55–57). ¶ Remember

that Taoism represents the dialogue between yin and yang in the emblem of a circle divided into equal fields of black and white, with a small dot of one colour embedded in its opposite field. As an illustration of balanced wholeness, this sign constructs the interaction of opposing forces within the closed constraints of a circular field. Paradoxically, the circularity of Taoist philosophy

subsumes difference into singularity (the circle), and Cage's later writing functions in a similar manner, because it provides a singular site for the existence of contradictory positions, without trying to synthesize those positions into a unified whole. From this dialogical perspective, we might revisit Julia Kristeva's consideration of the yin-yang interchange as a philosophy which goes beyond dualism (69), and her related suggestion that the dialogic ambivalence of poetic language is shared by the *tao*. Cage's later texts similarly destabilize the unity of definition that Kristeva associates with logic and scientific abstraction, because his

tao-inspired construction of a balance between quietism and activism parallels Kristeva's claim that any system based on a true-false or 'nothingness-notation' binary is unable to account for the operation of poetic language (70). Cage from the mid-1960s

does not question the relationship between binary terms such as nothingness and notation, but provides instead a notation of nothingness, a poetic language which expands to reference the silence within the social. ¶ Zhang Longxi has pointed out that the language of Taoism emphasizes 'the inadequacy and even futility of writing' (392). What is the purpose of engaging with the social

in writing, if the production of text is considered futile, and if, as the nineteenth-century commentator on Taoism Wei Yuan explains, the *tao* 'cannot be manifested through language'

(qtd. in Longxi 392)? Put differently, in terms set up by Cage: why will attempts to improve the world only make matters worse? For one thing, it seems that every historical overthrow of a repressive regime is followed by another form of repression. Saul Newman has argued that social organization is historically structured according to a repetition of power,

in the Lacanian sense – that is as a return of power, existing as a thing which can be studied in its own right and not merely as an epiphenomenon of capitalist economy or class relations. Power here is like the Lacanian Real, configured as 'that which returns to the same place,' an

'elusive lack that always resists symbolization by "returning"' (Newman 2). The Real of power is a lack or void which defies symbolization and is bound up with the constitution of subjectivity. It is therefore not to be

taken as an essence

or metaphysical presence (Newman 142). Cage's Zen-inspired 'nothing' parallels the Lacanian Real, because it exceeds linguistic definition. And to read Cage's 'nothing'

is to experience openness towards the Real, towards the void which cannot be signified. Unlike the Real of Power discussed by Newman, however, the Zen-Cage Real does not hinge on individual essence or a belief in the essentialism of the nation state. Instead of a 'Politics of the Real' we have in Cage a 'Nothing of the Real,' a paradoxical desire to speak from a position which escapes speech. ¶ A small step towards understanding the goal of Buddhist

desire *via* the route of psychoanalysis may

help clarify Cage's need for poetry as 'nothing.' In psychoanalytic terms, this form of 'nothing' functions as an *objet petit a*, a term which Lacan employs to represent 'a symbol

of the lack [. . .] in so far as it is lacking' (*Four* 103). Unlike the big O Other, which refers to the differential structure of language and social relations that produce the subject, the small o other is 'the object which can never be attained, which is really the cause of desire rather than that

towards which desire tends' (Evans 125). To obtain the *objet a* would be to eliminate the subject and the lack by which that subject is constituted: 'eradicating both in a radical negation that leaves behind no residue from which desire can start anew' (Ross 20). This negation illustrates why the *objet a* 'belongs to the psychic register of the Real which is beyond signification' (Jagodzinski 87), beyond

language and what can be thought, and consequently beyond subjectivity. For Lacan our subjectivity is constituted by the dialectic between lack

and desire, and to somehow put an end to desire would be to put an end to subjectivity itself. Moreover, because the subject of lack is born when it acquires language and takes up its place within a network of social relations, the absence of language would entail the absence of lack: the subject without lack would be speechless, silent, having nothing to say,

with nothing to think, and with no access to any form of differential structure setting it apart from anything else. In short, the individual subject would cease to exist – it would be blown out, so to speak, in the sense given by Buddhists to the

Sanskrit term *nirvāṇa*, which literally means a 'blowing out' of the fires and desires of greed, hatred and delusion. So that Cage's paradoxical articulation of a need for 'poetry as nothing' is really the expression of a desire for the subject-free zone of *nirvāṇa*, a non-space where all cravings and aversions have been completely eradicated. Cage's spatialized version of silence

performs as a new 'master signifier' – let's call it 'nothing,' but not in the sense given to that term by any dictionary – which is anarchistic, in as much as it provides a non-discursive parallel to the historical anarchists' critique of organized power, while concurrently surpassing the narrow, anarchist blind spot of essentialist individualism. ¶ Key elements

in Newman's account of modern power are the persistence of the nation state and the on-going legitimation of the essentialist individual. This first issue was addressed in 1970 by Cage when he claimed that 'anarchy is concerned only with the absence of government. And I believe that we would be able

to live much better than at present if we were in a world which contained no nations' (*For* 60). Newman argues that the frequent outbreak of wars over ethnicity and nationalism indicates how much we are still tied to the idea that ethnic and national identities should

have their own state (3), and Cage's anarchism here counters this prevalent cultural assumption. More pervasive for Newman is the continuing and essentialistic belief in personal identity, and this misconception has repercussions for any attempt at social reform or revolutionary

change. Ideologically constructed as a free, moral and rational subjectivity that is supposedly uncontaminated by power, the 'revolutionary' individual is in reality constituted by the

power that it seeks to overthrow. In other words, the place of resistance is actually the place of power, and consequently any social revolution is doomed to reaffirm the power it claims to oppose (Newman 5). As we have seen, the Buddhist concept of *anātman* forms one of the key bases of Cage's poetics, and his cultural production continually calls the notion

of an individual essence into question. From a Buddhist perspective, the largest 'national handicap' facing contemporary American society is the notion of a separate self, a notion which Philip Kapleau argues

is more securely fixed and vigorously asserted in the United States than anywhere else (379). The 'true self' for Zen is a no-self, which is empty of essence and void of individual identity, but which is infused with genuine compassion. Where American consumer culture was predicated on the

success of the individual, Cage's work refused individualism and self-expression altogether. Perhaps this is why his poetics appeared so scary,

so incomprehensible, and so boring, and why critics often responded to his work with such ridicule.[4] Cage's writing could thus be read as an antidote to American individualism, a Zen teaching tool to illustrate what happens when one abandons the complex relationships formed among the assumption of individual

essence, language and subjective lack – a seemingly impossible approach which is actually what transpires at the heart of Zen practice, where realization entails several simultaneous occurrences: 1) an understanding that the very idea of an individual self

has been a delusion all along; 2) a non-dualistic experience which cannot be symbolized in language; and 3) the cessation of desire, attachment and aversion.

As Marshall points out, Zen creates self-disciplined freedom rather than dependence on masters or priests, and enlightenment can only be achieved through self-effort. Zen is thus a significant precursor to modern anarchism, at least to the extent that its egalitarian ideal is 'shared by most anarchists who believe in the ultimate sovereignty of the individual'

(63). Paradoxically, in Zen, individual effort for enlightenment results in the realization that one is not really an individual at all, but exists instead as an organic whole with other so-called individuals and with nature.

¶ In his 1961 article 'Buddhist Anarchism,' Gary Snyder writes that although the major concerns of Buddhist philosophy are psychological and epistemological rather than historical or

sociological, no one can now afford to remain ignorant of the

nature of

contemporary governments, politics and social orders (1). As a remedy, Snyder advocates Zen meditation, which he claims can wipe out 'mountains of junk being pumped into the mind by mass media and supermarket universities' (1). Snyder's critique of the ideological state apparatuses yokes together the revolutionary practice of the West with the Asian practice of insight into

the 'basic self / void' (2). Once one clarifies the mind through meditation and realizes the mind's 'ego-driven anxieties and aggressions,' it

becomes possible to embody that realization, or

in Snyder's words, to bring it 'back out in the way you live, through personal

example and responsible action, ultimately towards the true community (*sangha*)[5] of "all beings"' (2). Underlying Snyder's article is a belief that the individual mind can achieve realization and liberation, and that realization leads to social

action. Zen anarchism is thus constructed as a personal response to social conditions rather than as the enforcement of an institutional agenda for social change. And this is precisely the anarchist logic we find in Cage's

writing, albeit with the meditation practice of Snyder replaced by the practice of writing, reading, and listening to 'nothing.' ¶ When asked by Daniel Charles about sound in traditional Zen music, Cage responded that 'Zen cultivates this flowing back towards

non-organization, that is, towards sounds as such, for and in themselves' (*For* 201). The non-organization of sounds and words is for Cage a microcosm of nature in her manner of operation, of social anarchy and of personal liberty. His long mesostic piece *Anarchy* (1988), for example, uses quotations about social reforms and the names of relevant authors as source texts, and then subjects these texts to a series of computer-generated chance operations to produce a highly fragmentary and disjunctive piece of writing. The first poem of the series uses the name of the 'anarchist prince' Peter Kropotkin as a mesostic spine:

        sPirit of
him for onE

      corporaTions
         arE
       failuRe
          Know-how of
         aRe
        idOls will

     free rePublic
    each thrOugh
        Them in
      maKe

        I
to me

       aNarchsm (1).

Notice that the penultimate line of the mesostic ('to me') is not incorporated into the name Kropotkin – perhaps a formal and critical indication of separation, with the 'me' of self standing in isolation, apart from the

nominally supported but syntactically distinct lines in the rest of the poem. Kropotkin's *Mutual Aid: A Factor of Evolution* (1901) is known as one of the seminal texts of modern anarchism. This text concludes by citing the 'earliest Buddhist and Christian communities'

as embodiments of 'the best aspects of mutual aid in early tribal life' (234). For Kropotkin, the ethical dimension of social evolution stems from one

person's love and support for another person, rather than from any form of institutional coercion or governmental dominance, and Buddhism provides him with an example of the earliest practice of mutual aid (234). With its roots in Taoist and Buddhist philosophy and experience, Cage's anarchism is highly sympathetic to Kropotkin's valuation of shared

support over shared struggle. And like so much of Cage's writing, the fragmentary character of *Anarchy* recalls his Zen-based cultivation of non-organization, in which all phenomena are considered interdependent, mutually accommodating, and non-hierarchical in value. Yet *Anarchy* differs from earlier texts such as the lecture-poems collected in *Silence* and *Empty Words* because of its direct and explicit use of political statements about anarchism as source texts, including not only Kropotkin but also Thoreau's statement: '[t]hat government is best which governs not at all,' the early twentieth-century anarchist Emma Goldman's claim that: '[t]he problem

that confronts us today, and

the nearest future is to solve, is how to be oneself and yet in oneness with others,' and Cage's own writing about anarchy: '[p]rivate prospect of enlightenment's no longer sufficient. Not just self- but social realization' (*Anarchy*

viii, viii). ¶ Aside from holding a brief interest in Mao during the 1970s,[6] Cage remained

committed to his particular brand of Taoist and Zen-based anarchism, in both his cultural production and in his social views, from the mid-

1960s until his death. One could say that the shift in Cage's desire for self-enlightenment towards social-realization parallels the historic shift in Buddhist philosophy which occurred in the first centuries C. E. Cage's early work echoes the founding *Theravada* Buddhist teachings, in which the aspirant seeks enlightenment as a so-called *Arhat* who will never be re-born, but whose subjectivity will be extinguished entirely in *Nirvana*. On the other hand, Cage's later concern with social change echoes the *Bodhisattva* ideal of the *Mahāyāna* tradition, in which the aspirant vows to return for many lives in order to

benefit all sentient beings through compassionate action. In any case, Cage acknowledges in the introduction

to *Anarchy* that his fragmentary use of source materials does not make ordinary sense, although it could be thought of as music, or following Marshall McLuhan, as information brushing against information (vi).[7] The disjunctive character of this piece thus prompted Cage to call it 'an anarchic

text on anarchy' (qtd. in Cruice 15). He does, however, acknowledge that his creation of a performative link between anarchist philosophy and aesthetic texts is complicated. In an interview with Joan Retallack conducted in 1992, the year of his death and four years after the publication of *Anarchy*, he claimed that we may be able to address our individual experiences in the world of art, although we have more difficulty doing so in the

'real world' (*Musicage* 207). It might seem

puzzling that Cage

would construct such a dualistic

opposition between the real world and the world of art so late in his life, after so much of his cultural production had attempted to break down that very boundary. Yet his reflexivity in this area articulates one of the central problems facing

the politicized artist: how does one intervene

in the dominant culture without participating in the forms of production legitimated by the

dominant culture? Or in

the Buddhist context, how does individual realization impinge on the wider social situation? Perhaps, Cage here simply

points out the contradictions inherent in political activism. That such a question might be asked signals an opposition to the limitations of political fundamentalism, or to any discourse which dis-functions through the

eradication of inquiry and dialogue. Clearly, this form of non-questioning, political monoculture is contrary to the expansive space of nature, anarchy and aesthetics that Cage's work sought to establish. ¶ Regardless of Cage's uncertainty about the contradiction between life and art, his politicized Buddhist-environmentalist poetic can be distinguished from the sort

of social activism described by Vietnamese Buddhist monk Thich (Venerable) Nhat Hanh and others as 'engaged Buddhism.' Hanh advocates a mindful approach to social responsibility, and has led retreats for marginalized social groups such as Vietnam war veterans, prison inmates, political prisoners and refugees, as well as with more mainstream participants such as mental health and social workers, members of the American congress, and

representatives from both sides of the Palestinian/Israeli conflict. Hanh's approach to political

struggle is to bring mindful awareness to every situation, not only to formal sitting or walking meditation practice, but also to the social spheres of education, the government and the corporate world. He advises heads of state to 'practice peace,' to pray for peace

before being effective in asking other heads of state to 'join in making peace' (*Answers* 97). Where Hanh wants to

train political and corporate leaders to be more mindful in conducting their state and business activities, Cage desires an

end to government altogether. And although both Cage and Hanh uphold a socially responsible role for the artist that is based on the Buddhist experience of 'interpenetration' (Cage) or 'interbeing' (Hanh),[8] the latter's aesthetics could not be further removed from Cage. In

the poem 'Please Call Me By My True Name' (1991), for example, Hanh writes: 'Look deeply: every second I am arriving / to be a bud on a spring branch, / to be a tiny bird, with small fragile wings' (121). The poem continues with the speaker self-identifying with natural imagery such as a caterpillar, a stone, a mayfly,

a frog, and 'the grass snake / that silently feeds upon the frog' (122). This natural imagery shifts, however, to incorporate social significance: 'I am the child of Uganda, all skin and bones [. . . .] I am the twelve-year-old girl, / refugee on a small boat [. . . .] I am a

member of the politburo' (124). Bradley F. Clough remarks that this poem shows a 'deep identity with the life of natural beings, even with inanimate life forms such as a stone' (124), and that Hanh's understanding of interrelated natural and social phenomena offers him

a way to develop mindful compassion, even for others who cause war 'because they too are caught in its web of pain' (125). Although Hanh's poetics draw heavily on his Zen-based understanding of non-dualism, his language use remains representational, and does not move beyond a dualistic distinction between signifier and signified. That

is to say, his representation of oneness among the natural and the social provides us with a conventional, common-sense articulation of the theme of inter-being, and for all its social engagement, the poem does not produce a lived experience of the empty, absolute nothing or void which is beyond thought and description, and which is the underlying

ground or Real experienced during Zen training. Historically, Zen masters have used absurd and sometimes violent tactics to shock their students into realization, and Cage's employment of entropological poetics, chance operations, illegibility, indeterminacy and

Zen-like anecdotes provides a similar challenge to conventional patterns of thought and experience. 'sworn Poet of / libeRty,' he writes in *Anarchy*, 'nOthing to / pieces Before it / sociaL' (2); the poem continues

in this disjunctive manner for eighty-one pages. Unlike

Hanh's lyrical approach to Buddhist poetics, Cage's mesostic reconfiguration of conventional syntax sidesteps the thematic rationale which constructs inter-being at the level of content – in fact, Cage's entropological texts short-circuit instrumental reason altogether in favour of a non-conceptual experience of emptiness. While the Buddhist experience of non-duality, emptiness and compassion underpins the writing of both poets, their aesthetic approach to this experience is radically different. ¶ Ultimately Cage's entropological and anarchist poetics do not present a well-constructed blueprint for an alternative to the social order and the related environmental degradation of the late twentieth century. What his writing does provide, however, is a micro-site which foregrounds a lived experience of social anarchism and nature in the manner of its operation.

This experience differs from conceptual notions of anarchy and environmentalism. Cage's green-anarchist poetics offer us a plenitude of experience, a transformation of our sense

of what constitutes the Real – or rather, a sense of how the Real cannot be constituted, conceptualized or reified in any way. Cage's Buddhist nature poetics serve as the site for a specific sub-culture of readers to collectively organize affect and knowledge. Such work indicates the presence of a new form of social organization which replaces

the subject's misrecognition of consciousness as being fully individualized and

autonomous, with the more flexible and conscious enjoyment of a collective social bond

based on non-meaning – that is, based on language which does not communicate knowledge, which does not require the interpretative skills of someone trained in close reading, which sets up an entropological continuum between subjectivity and the phenomena of nature, and which does not bolster up a fictive sense of unified subjectivity. What was the social challenge expressed by Cage's Zen-influenced ecopoetics? This question might be answered with reference to Žižek's remarks on ethnicity and the new political situations in Eastern Europe. Žižek reads the struggle between ethnic groups not only as a clash between

different symbolic organizations, but also between different relationships towards enjoyment, or *jouissance*. This type of enjoyment is not the same as pleasure, because it denotes the 'paradoxical satisfaction procured by a painful encounter with a *Thing* that perturbs the equilibrium of the 'pleasure principle' (*Tarrying*

280). Enjoyment does not stem from unpleasure avoided, but from the subject's relationship towards its own objectified lack or void in the form of the *Thing* – that is, towards an

object

that materializes the nothingness experienced by the desiring subject. For Žižek, nations function as sublimated materializations of the *Thing*. Nations are structured through the organization of enjoyment (as a response to lack) in cultural practices such as feasts, rituals of mating and initiation ceremonies. Enjoyment is the non-discursive element that 'appears' to subjects through these practises: a nation 'exists only

as long as its specific enjoyment continues to be materialized in a set of social practices and transmitted through national myths that structure these practices' (*Tarrying* 202). Drawing a structural parallel between the enjoyment of nations

and the enjoyment of different poetic forms and contexts, it would appear that readers of the voice-based identity poetics of the traditional lyric poem enjoy the *Thing* of the well-crafted poem, which assumes a unitary, individualistic subjectivity for its construction, and which comes into being through repressing

excessive, non-discursive affect. Instead of crafting the poem as a

Thing for the enjoyment of knowledge, personal expression and unified consciousness, Cage's work embraces an affective, non-discursive *jouissance* of non-meaning. Paradoxically, the *Thing* about Cage is a

plenitude of nothing, an expression of the void materialized in language. As such, his writing offered readers the means to organize their enjoyment and to foster a new and alternative social bond. This bond was structured not only by the innovative and experimental writing tactics of the post-war period, but also by the presence of Buddhism, political anarchism and ecological activism, which here took on a critical

role because they were so absolutely *other* to the cultural practices and social organization of the American dream. ¶ In the 1972 foreword to *M: Writings '67–'72*, Cage cites Norman O. Brown's claim that syntax is the arrangement of the army, and that as we

move away from syntax, 'we demilitarize language' (n.p.). Brown and Cage employed this metaphor for language during a period when America was still enmeshed in an increasingly unpopular war in Vietnam; the demilitarized zone between North and South Vietnam was an

area which by treaty was not supposed to permit any military activity, although in reality it was bombed by the Americans, clustered with land mines, and used as a battleground at various points during the war. In theory a DMZ functions like a neutral territory, free from the administration and control on either side of its borders. To

present the non-

syntactic use of language as a form of DMZ is to metaphorically compare linguistic freedom with social revolution:

'[w]e begin to actually live together, and the thought of separating doesn't enter our minds' (*M* n.p.). Cage further writes that in his texts 'Nonsense and silence are produced' in a manner

that he claims is 'familiar to lovers' (*M* n.p.). Love, the absence of borders, Buddhist silence and non-separation: perhaps the DMZ of Cagean

language and its support for an all-encompassing social and aesthetic revolt could be historicized as the construction of a salvational story – a desire for Utopia which owes as much to the social context of the late 1960s and early 1970s as it does to Cage's long-standing interests

in ecology and Zen. What is

remarkable about Cage, however, is that it is possible to chart this impulse in his writing

throughout his career, and not just as a response to the increased interest in music and art as expedient means towards non-violent social revolution – an interest which formed one of the key ideological perspectives for the 'peace and love' counter culture of the baby-boomer generation. As early as

1947, for example, Cage claimed that the purpose of music was to fill one 'with peace and love' (*Silence* 62), while as late as a 1990 interview with Joan Retallack he optimistically stated that in one hundred years

from now our social problems 'will be recognized by everyone and people will put their minds to solving them and we'll *do* it!' (*Musicage* 44). It is a happy thing that Cage ends one of his final interviews with laughter.

Endnotes

The imitation of nature in her manner of operation

1 In a short letter from Cage to the pianist David Tudor, written while Tudor was living at Black Mountain College in August of 1951, Cage writes: 'By the way there's a poet down there forwarding reading matters: (books follow) Charles Olson if he's any good it would be marvellous, in dire need of poetry.' (MS. David Tudor Papers, Getty Archive, Los Angeles).

2 The Japanese word *kōan* literally means 'public document' or 'authoritative statute.' Suzuki's *An Introduction to Zen Buddhism* (1949) describes the *kōan* as an anecdote, dialogue, question, or statement which the Zen student meditates upon in order to attain the truth of Zen (102). While adherents of other schools of Buddhism practice meditation, *kōan* practice is unique to Zen.

3 Kōun Yamada Roshi glosses the imagery of the horse and whip as a simile taken from the *Anguttara Nikāya*, where 'where Buddha compares people to four kinds of horses. The first are those that start even at the shadow of a whip and perform the will of the horseman [. . . .] These similes are meant to indicate the depth of each individual's causal relation to the Dharma and also the degree of aspiration on the part of the student' (159).

4 More recent Buddhist scholars and religious practitioners similarly agree that the term *śūnyatā* cannot be adequately explained or even described because it is entirely other to the conditioned world of cause and effect. See, for example, Robert Thurman's characterization of emptiness as a 'pure negation of the ultimate existence of anything [. . .] a concept descriptive of the ultimate reality through its pure negation of whatever may be supposed to be ultimately real' (160), or the contemporary Western Buddhist teacher Sangharakshita's description of *śūnyatā* as 'the entire emptiness or voidness of all conceptual activity' (*Clearing* 67).

5 David Revill points out that Cage preferred Dada to Surrealism because, as Cage puts it, 'Surrealism relates to therapy, whereas Dada relates to religion' (125).

6 The Zen experience of 'seeing into one's own nature' is perhaps best exemplified in *Silence* and elsewhere in Cage's *oeuvre* though his use of 'chance operations.' The crucial point of using chance operations in relation to Zen's dismantling of the autonomous ego is that chance limits authorial control and calls for an acceptance of the situation at hand: '[t]he *I Ching* says that if you don't accept the chance operations you have no right to use them. Which is very clear, so that's what I do' (Cage 'Taking' 11). By limiting subjective agency, Cage opens up the possibility for something like the *kenshō* experience of 'seeing into one's own nature' – that is, into an experience that is not delineated by boundaries of the individual ego, and not located in a single consciousness which distinguishes between me and you, but which perceives the mutual 'interpenetration' of all things.

7 Cf. the Tibetan word *spros bral* or 'indeterminable,' a term – used in the *Dzogchen* Buddhist tradition to indicate an experience which is incapable of elaboration and which is free from conceptual limitations or restrictions to a single meaning (Dowman 187). Cage had several books on this form of Buddhism in his personal library.

8 In a commemorative lecture delivered to the Inamori Foundation in 1989 on the occasion of his winning the Kyoto Prize, Cage remarked that he thought of Nāgārjuna as an uncompromising Buddhist philosopher, the 'Malevich of Buddhist philosophy' ('Autobiographical' 4).

9 Cage referred to a series of his musical compositions with titles indicating their durations (e.g. '26'1.1499') as 'The Ten Thousand Things' (Pritchett 95).

10 Cage remembers studying with Suzuki at Columbia University in the late 1940s, yet the Zen teacher actually moved to New York in 1950, first lectured at Columbia in 1951, and began teaching regularly there in 1952 (Gann 103).

11 This poem is often attributed to Bodhidharma, the semi-legendary first patriarch of *Ch'an*. Most likely Cage encountered the poem in one of Suzuki's lectures, or in his 1949 book *Essays on Zen Buddhism*, where Suzuki writes that it 'sums up all that is claimed by Zen as religion' (20).

12 Cf. Alan Watts' *Beat Zen, Square Zen, and Zen* (1959), where Watts criticizes Cage's use of Zen in order to 'justify the indiscriminate framing of simply anything' (11). Watts argues that Cage forsook his earlier interest in the prepared piano to confront audiences with random noises, and this confrontation is closer to therapy than to art (12). In contrast to Cage's approach, Watts cites the Zen practice of 'controlling accidents' in poetry, painting and ceramics, where 'the accidental is always recognized in relation to what is ordered and controlled,' and he further upholds the Zen artist's revelation of

'nature through accidents in a context of highly disciplined art' (15). Incidentally, Cage later claimed that Watts changed his mind after he read *Silence* (*For* 107)!

13 In 'Buddhism and Ecology' (2000) Harris contrasts Suzuki's approach with the Judeo-Christian 'mastery' of nature, and points to how Suzuki's perspective on Zen 'naturalism' came to affect the initial stages of Western ecological discourse. See also Grosnick (1994) for a discussion of early Buddhist controversy on the issue of the Buddhahood of non-sentient objects. This controversy was not shared by Zen.

14 The so-called 'deep ecology' movement shares some affinities with Buddhist thought, because the movement identifies 'the dualistic separation of humans from nature promoted by Western philosophy and culture as the origin of the environmental crisis,' and demands 'a return to a monistic, primal identification of humans and the ecosphere' (Garrard 21).

15 Specifically, Skinner cites Finlay's poetry garden Little Sparta, Cayley's electronic textual transformations, Cecelia Vicuña's etymological ruminations, Ronald Johnson's concrete poetry, and Cage's 'writing through' Thoreau. See also Skinner's 'Thoughts on Things: Poetics of the Third Landscape' (2010) for a discussion of Smithson's consideration of Claude Lèvi-Strauss, the structural anthropologist who coined the term entropology as an alternative to anthropology.

16 Along with his representation of nature, Thoreau was also interested in Buddhist philosophy and compassion: 'I know that some will have hard thoughts of me, when they hear their Christ named beside my Buddha,' he writes in *A Week on the Concord and Merrimack Rivers* (1849) 'yet I am sure that I am willing they should love their Christ more than my Buddha, for the love is the main thing' (67).

17 I am borrowing the term 'recycles' in this context from Harriet Tarlo, who points out that the 'recycling' of found text is particularly prevalent in 'experimental poetry which has a philosophical or political engagement with the environment and/or ecology' (115). In ecological terms, the recycling of found text could further be reconsidered as a strident critique of the disposable goods which our economic situation consistently produces, and which consumer culture uses without regard for environmental sustainability.

18 In entropological terms, however, is interesting to note that Cage's purposeful purposelessness differs in tone from what Jennifer Roberts has labelled as Smithson's 'interest in disinterest.' Roberts points out that Smithson was attracted to themes of lethargy, listlessness, tedium, and stagnation and that his 'interest in disinterest is perhaps most easily explained by his fascination with entropy and its accompanying cosmic exhaustion' (101). Where

Smithson finds exhaustion in the entropic transformation of the universe, Cage finds a highly affirmative sense of playfulness and humour, a big 'Yes to our presence together in chaos' (*Silence* 195). Cage's cheerfully entropological writing represents, in a highly material manner, the Zen experience of emptiness.

19 It may be interesting to note that psychoanalysis also sets a precedent for thinking about the recycling of found text, such as can be seen in Cage's 'writing-through' of Thoreau or Joyce. Freud used the term 'ready-made' for the recycling of earlier textual material at least six years before Duchamp's first ready-made sculpture, and Freud's ideas about writing may be able to clarify some of the impetus behind Cage's recycling practice. In 'Creative Writers and Daydreaming' (first delivered as a lecture in 1907), Freud outlines two types of creative writing. He makes a distinction between, on the one hand, writers who 'seem to originate their own material,' and on the other hand, writers who, in his own words, 'take over their material ready-made' (152). Freud's analysis centres on writers who originate their own material, which he argues is like a type of daydream, a continuation of and substitute for what was once the play of childhood (152). However, it is significant that Freud also mentions the ready-made use of text. He argues that we must not neglect to go back to the 'kind of imaginative works which we have to recognize, not as original creations, but as the re-fashioning of ready-made, familiar material' (152). Freud goes on to psychoanalyse the rationale behind the intertextual recycling of material by claiming that the writer still keeps a certain amount of independence, which can express itself in the choice of material and in the way that material is changed and assimilated. For Freud, it is also highly probable that work derived from the 'popular treasure house of myths, legends and fairy tales [. . .] are distorted vestiges of the wishful fantasies of whole nations' (152). What is key here is a turn away from the purely individual, towards an investigation of the social in psychoanalytical terms. Although Freud has in mind the intertextual re-casting of myth by 'the ancient authors of epics and tragedies' (149), we could extend his brief words on the ready-made use of text to the practice of found poetry, which functions through the recycling of already existing textual material. To focus on this perspective is to move beyond a concentration on the individual writer's psyche, broadening the scope to consider psycho-social conditions – or in the case of Cage's Buddhist poetics, the entirety of social, environmental and cosmological conditions.

20 See for example Kosuth's influential essay 'Art After Philosophy' (1969): 'the propositions of art are not factual, but linguistic in character – that is, they do not describe the behaviour of physical or

even mental objects; they express definitions of art, or the formal consequences of definitions of art' (7).
21 Wildness and excitement is considered by Buddhists to be one of the five hindrances or impediments (*nīvaraṇa*) to meditation practice. The other four hindrances are: desire, malice, depression and sloth, and doubt.
22 This quotation comes from the prominent sixth-century *Ch'an* poem 'Verses on the Faith of Mind' by Seng-t'san (Sosan in Japanese), a text which may have been known to Cage through Suzuki's translation, which I quote here.
23 Cage often supported interfaith dialogue, citing as a precedent the teachings of the Hindu sage Ramakrishna, 'who said all religions are the same, like a lake to which people who are thirsty come from different directions, calling its water by different names' ('Autobiographical' 3).

Not just self- but social realization

1 Cage remarked in a 1987 interview with Peter Dickinson that his single attempt at analysis was with a 'Jungian, I think recommended by Joseph Campbell' (35).
2 See Craig Dworkin's *Reading the Illegible* (2003) for an analysis of poetic illegibility. Dworkin argues that Cage and other producers of 'illegible' poetic texts 'disrupt the message [and] unsettle the code of the status quo,' thereby setting up the 'potential for new social and political orders' (39). While Dworkin acknowledges that his critical approach is not without historical and contemporary precedents, his specific focus on illegibility is particularly relevant to Cage's poetics. Dworkin looks to Guy Debord and the *Internationale Situationniste* to explicate the ideological force behind the appropriation of source texts and the unreadable quality of much formally innovative writing. Key to his discussion is Debord's suggestion that radical texts disrupt the traditional 'conduit' model of communication in which an addresser constructs and transmits information to a receptive and passive addressee. For Debord, 'true communication' occurs when the distinction between addresser and addressee disappears, when readers become 'both producer and consumer' (qtd. in Dworkin 11). For Debord (and Dworkin) this new model of reading politicizes the reading experience: '[o]ne never really contests an organization of existence without contesting all of that organization's forms of language' (qtd. in Dworkin 163). The socially radical aspect of Cage's writing occurs

when his texts turn to indeterminacy, incomprehensibility and silence – when they become, in Dworkin's terms, illegible.

3. Cage here moves away from Suzuki's limited presentation of the Rinzai sect of Zen. See Leonard's *Into the Light of Things* (1994) for a detailed discussion of how Suzuki focused almost exclusively on the sudden school associated with Rinzai, and how later Western Zen commentators have criticized his early work for this omission (147–62).

4. Cage was frequently charged with charlatanism; in a 1960 letter to David Tudor about his performance of 'Water Walk' on the American television game show 'I've Got a Secret,' Cage writes: '[e]verybody it seems was delighted all the way from artists to street cleaners. No doubt critics just as furious as ever. They now complain that I'm a proponent of a Capitalist society' (MS. David Tudor Papers, Getty Institute, Los Angeles). See http://www.youtube.com/watch?v=SSulycqZH-U for a recording of this performance.

5. *Sangha* is the Buddhist term for 'association' or 'community.' Usually it refers to the monastic community of ordained monks or nuns, but it can also refer to all of the Buddha's followers. This later usage is more common in the West.

6. Like many liberals during the Vietnam War, Cage was drawn to Maoism, although he later repudiated Maoist philosophy because it depended on 'power militarism' and because it concerned a single nation rather than the entire earth (Silverman 269).

7. Cage's interest in anarchism was overdetermined by the influence of thinkers such as Marshall McCluhan and Buckminster Fuller (among others), although the religious impetus discussed here remained central to his politics throughout his late career.

8. Hanh has coined the term 'interbeing' to account for the not-dualistic character of phenomenon: 'To be' is to inter-be. You cannot just be by yourself alone' ('Interbeing' 208).

Works cited

Acconci, Vito. 'Contacts/Contexts (Frame of Reference).' *0-9* 6 (1969): 17–26.
Adam, Michael. *Wandering in Eden: Three Ways to the East Within Us*. New York: Knopf, 1976.
Allen, Donald, Ed. *The New American Poetry 1945–1960*. New York: Grove, 1960.
Ashbery, John. *The Tennis Court Oath*. Middletown: Wesleyan UP, 1962.
Bachelard, Gaston. The Poetics of Space. 1958. Boston: Beacon P, 1994.
Bal, Mieke. *Travelling Concepts in the Humanities: A Rough Guide*. Toronto: U of Toronto P, 2002.
Basho, Matsuo. http://www.brainyquote.com/quotes/authors/m/matsuo_basho.html. Accessed on February 10, 2011.
Bataille, Georges. *The Absence of Myth: Writings on Surrealism*. Trans. Michael Richardson. London: Verso, 1994.
—. *Literature and Evil*. 1957. Trans. Alastair Hamilton. London: Calder and Boyars, 1973.
Batchelor, Martine. 'Even the Stones Smile: Selections from the Scriptures.' *Buddhism and Ecology*. Eds. Martine Batchelor and Kerry Brown. London: Cassel, 1992, 2–17.
Batchelor, Stephen. 'The Sands of the Ganges: Notes Towards a Buddhist Ecological Philosophy.' *Buddhism and Ecology*. Eds. Martine Batchelor and Kerry Brown. London: Cassel, 1992, 31–39.
Beckett, L.C. *Neti Neti (Not This Not That)*. London: The Ark P, 1955.
Bernstein, Charles. *A Poetics*. London: Harvard UP, 1992.
Berrigan, Ted. 'The Business of Writing Poetry.' *Talking Poetics From Naropa Institute: Annals of the Jack Kerouac School of Disembodied Poetics, Volume One*. Eds. Anne Waldman and Marilyn Webb. Boston: Shambhala, 1978, 39–62.
—. 'Interview with John Cage' 1966. *Against Expression: An Anthology of Conceptual Writing*. Eds. Craig Dworkin and Kenneth Goldsmith. Evanston: Northwestern UP, 2011.
—. *The Sonnets*. New York: 'C' Press, 1964.
Blofeld, John [Chu Chàn], trans. *The Huang Po Doctrine of Universal Mind*. London: The Buddhist Society, 1947.
Bloom, Ina. 'Signal to Noise.' *Artforum* 48.6 (2010): 170–175.

Bryson, J. Scott. 'Introduction.' *Ecopoetry: A Critical Introduction.* Salt Lake City: University of Utah P, 2002, 1–13.
Cage, John. *I–IV.* Cambridge: Harvard UP, 1990.
—. '_____, _____ _____ Circus on _____' *Roaratoriao: An Irish Circus on Finnegan's Wake.* Ed. Klaus Schoening. Koeningstein: Atheneum Verlag, 1985, 172–175.
—. *Anarchy.* Middletown: Wesleyan UP, 1988.
—. 'An Autobiographical Statement.' http://johncage.org/autobiographical_statement.html. Accessed September 28, 2011.
—. 'An Interview with John Cage.' With John Held, Jr. http://www.mailartist.com/johnheldjr/CageInterview.html. Accessed November 3, 2010.
—. *A Year From Monday: New Lectures and Writings.* Middletown: Wesleyan UP, 1968.
—. *Empty Words: Writing '73–'78.* Middletown: Wesleyan UP, 1978.
—. 'Form is a Language.' 1960. *John Cage: An Anthology.* Ed. Richard Kostelanetz. New York: Da Capo P, 1970, 135.
—. *For the Birds: In Conversation with Daniel Charles.* London: Marion Boyars, 1981.
—. 'Interview with Peter Dickinson, BBC Studios, New York City, June 29, 1987.' *Cage Talk: Dialogues With and About John Cage.* Ed. Peter Dickinson. Rochester: Rochester UP, 2006, 25–51.
—. 'John Cage.' Interview with Cole Gagne and Tracy Carras. *Soundpieces: Interviews with American Composers.* London: Scarecrow P, 1982, 70–86.
—. 'John Cage: Empty Words with Relevant Material.' *Talking Poetics From Naropa Insitute: Annals of the Jack Kerouac School of Disembodied Poetics*, Vol. 1. Eds. Anne Waldman and Marilyn Webb. Boulder and London: Shambhala, 1978.
—. 'Letter to David Tudor', August 1951. MS. David Tudor Papers. The Getty Institute, Los Angeles.
—. 'Letter to David Tudor' N.D., probably 1960. MS. David Tudor Papers. The Getty Institute, Los Angeles.
—. 'List No. 2.' 1961. *John Cage: An Anthology.* Ed. Richard Kostelanetz. New York: Da Capo P, 1970, 138–139.
—. *M: Writings '67–'72.* Middletown: Wesleyan UP, 1973.
—. *Musicage: Cage Muses on Word Art Music.* Ed. Joan Retallack. Middletown: Wesleyan UP, 1996.
—. 'Overpopulation and Art.' *John Cage: Composed in America.* Eds. Marjorie Perloff and Charles Junkerman. Chicago: U of Chicago P, 1994, 14–38.
—. *Silence.* Middletown: Wesleyan UP, 1961.
—. 'Taking Chances: Laurie Anderson and John Cage.' *Tricycle: A Buddhist Review* 1.4 (1992): 10–12.

—. 'Water Walk.' *I've Got a Secret.* WFMU 1960. http://www.youtube.com/watch?v=SSulycqZH-U. Accessed June 2011.
—. 'Where'm'Now.' *Beneath a Single Moon: Buddhism in Contemporary American Poetry.* Eds. Kent Johnson and Craig Paulenich. Boston: Shambhala, 1991, 43–44.
—. *Writings Through Finnegan's Wake.* New York: Printed Editions, 1978.
—. *X: Writings '79–'82.* Middletown: Wesleyan UP, 1987.
Chandrakanthan, A.J.V. 'The Silence of Buddha and his Contemplation of the Truth.' *Spirituality Today* 40.2 (1988): 145–156.
Christensen, Paul. 'Philip Whalen.' *The Beats: Literary Bohemians in Post-war America.* Ed. Ann Charters. *Dictionary of Literary Biography*, Vol. 16. Chicago: Gale, 1983, 554–572.
Clark, Tom. Rev. of *OVERTIME: Selected Poems of Philip Whalen. Jacket* 7. http://jacketmagazine.com/07/whalen-clark.html. Accessed June 30, 2011.
Cleary, Thomas. *Zen Antics: 100 Stories of Enlightenment.* Boston: Shambhala, 1993.
Clough, Bradley S. 'Altruism in Contemporary Buddhism: Thich Nhat Hanh's Socially Engaged Buddhism.' *Altruism in World Religions.* Eds. Jacob Neusner and Bruce Chilton. Washington: Georgetown UP, 2005.
Coomaraswamy, Ananda. *The Transformation of Nature in Art.* Cambridge MA: Harvard UP, 1934.
Cruice, Valerie. 'Wesleyan Symposium Celebrates Cage.' Connecticut Weekly. *The New York Times.* February 21, 1988, CN 15.
Curtin, Deane. 'Dōgen, Deep Ecology, and the Ecological Self.' *Environmental Ethics* 16 (1994): 195–213.
Deleuze, Gilles and Felix Guattari. *A Thousand Plateaus: Capitalism and Schizophrenia.* 1980. Trans. Brian Massumi. Minneapolis: Minnesota UP, 1987.
Dōgen. *Moon in a Dewdrop: Writings of Zen Master Dogen* [*Shōbōgenzō*]. Ed. Kazuaki Tanahashi. Trans. Robert Aitken and Kazuaki Tanahashi et al. Longmead, Dorset: Element Books, 1988.
Dowman, Keith. *The Flight of the Garuda: The Dzogchen Tradition of Tibetan Buddhism.* Trans. Keith Dowman. Somerville: Wisdom Publications, 2003.
Dworkin, Craig. *Reading the Illegible.* Evanston: Avant-Garde and Modernism Series, Northwestern University Press, 2003.
Dworkin, Craig and Kenneth Goldsmith, Eds. *Against Expression: An Anthology of Conceptual Writing.* Evanston: Northwestern UP, 2011.
Eckhart, Meister. 'Works Inward and Outward.' 1440. *The Works of Meister Eckhart Doctor Ecstaticus.* Vol. II. Trans. C. de B. Evans. London: John M. Watkins, 1931, 36–42.

Evans, Dylan. *An Introductory Dictionary of Lacanian Psychoanalysis*. New York: Routledge, 1996.

Falk, Jane. 'Finger Pointing at the Moon: Zen and the Poetry of Philip Whalen.' *The Emergence of Buddhist American Literature*. Eds. John Whalen-Bridge and Gary Storhoff. Albany: SUNY P, 2009, 103–122.

Fink, Bruce. 'The Master Signifier and the Four Discourses.' In *Key Concepts of Lacanian Psychoanalysis*. Ed. Dany Nobus. New York: Other P, 1999, 29–47.

Fitterman, Robert. *Rob the Plagiarist*. New York: Roof Books, 2009.

Freud, Sigmund. 'Creative Writers and Day Dreaming.' 1907. *The Standard Edition of the Complete Psychological Works*. Trans. James Strachey. London: Hogarth P, 1953.

—. 1901. *The Interpretation of Dreams*. Trans. James Strachey. Hammondsworth: Penguin, 1976.

Frost, Elisabeth A. 'Leslie Scalapino.' *American Poets Since W.W. II*, 6th Series. Ed. Joseph Conte. *Dictionary of Literary Biography*, Vol. 193. Detroit: Gale, 1998, 318-572-328.

Gallop, Jane. *Reading Lacan*. Ithaca: Cornell UP, 1985.

Gann, Kyle. *No Such Thing as Silence: John Cage's 4'33"*. New Haven: Yale UP, 2010.

Garrard, Greg. *Ecocriticism*. London: Routledge, 2004.

Gifford, Terry. 'Gary Snyder and the Post-Pastoral.' *Ecopoetry: A Critical Introduction*. Ed. J. Scott Bryson. Salt Lake City: U of Utah P, 2002, 77–87.

Ginsberg, Allen. *Howl and Other Poems*. San Francisco: City Lights, 1956.

—. 'Meditation and Poetics' 1988. *Beneath a Single Moon: Buddhism in Contemporary American Poetry*. Eds. Kent Johnson and Craig Paulenich. Boston: Shambhala, 1991, 94–100.

—. 'Why I Meditate.' *Collected Poems 1947–1997*. New York: HarperCollins, 2006, 851.

Glass, N. Robert. '*The Tibetan Book of the Dead*: Deleuze and the Positivity of the Second Light.' *Deleuze and Religion*. Ed. Mary Bryden. London: Routledge, 2001, 65–75.

Grosnick, William. 'The Buddhahood of the Grasses and the Trees: Ecological Sensitivity or Scriptural Understanding.' *An Ecology of the Spirit: Religious Reflection and Environmental Consciousness*. Ed. Michael Barnes. Langham: UP of America, 1994, 197–208.

Goldsmith, Kenneth. 'Being Boring.' *Séance*. Eds. Christine Wertheim and Matias Viegener. Los Angeles: Make New P, 2006, 67–72.

—. 'Why Conceptual Writing? Why Now?' *Against Expression: Contemporary Conceptual Poetics*. Eds. Kenneth Goldsmith and Craig Dworkin. Evanston, IL: Northwestern University Press, 2011, xvii–xxii.

Hanh, Thich Nhat. *Answers From the Heart: Practical Responses to Life's Burning Questions.* Berkley: Parallax P, 2009.
—. 'Interbeing'. 1988. *What Book!? Buddha Poems From Beat to Hiphop.* Ed. Gary Gach. Berkeley: Parallax P, 1998, 208–209.
—. 'Please Call Me By My True Name.' *Peace is Every Step: The Path of Mindfulness in Everyday Life.* New York: Bantam Books, 1991, 121–124.
Harris, Ian. 'Buddhism and Ecology.' *Contemporary Buddhist Ethics.* Ed. Damien Keown. Richmond: Curzon, 2000, 113–135.
Hart, Kevin. *The Trespass of the Sign: Deconstruction, Theology and Philosophy.* Cambridge: Cambridge UP, 1989.
Hilson, Jeff. 'Homophonic Translation: Sense and Sound.' *Music, Text and Translation.* Ed. Helen Julia Minors. London: Continuum P, 2012, 95–106.
Holquist, Michael. 'Bakhtin and the Body.' *Critical Studies* 1.2. (1989): 19–42.
Humphreys, Christmas. *The Wisdom of Buddhism.* 1960. London: Rider and Company, 1970.
Jagodzinski, Jan. 'The Ethics of the 'Real' in Levinas, Lacan, and Buddhism: Pedagogical Implications.' *Educational Theory* 52.1 (2002): 81–96.
Jakobson, Roman. 'On Linguistic Aspects of Translation.' *On Translation.* Ed. R.A. Brower. 232–239. Cambridge: Harvard UP, 1959.
Jay, Martin. *Downcast Eyes: The Denigration of Vision in Twentieth-Century French Thought.* Berkeley: U of California P, 1994.
Jung, C.G. 'Forward to Suzuki's "Introduction to Zen Buddhism."' *Collected Works of C.G. Jung, Volume 11: Psychology and Religion: West and East.* Eds. and Trans. Gerhard Adler and R.F.C. Hull. Princeton: Princeton UP, 1970, 538–557.
Kahn, Douglas. *Noise, Water, Meat: A History of Sound in the Arts.* Cambridge, MA: The MIT Press, 1999.
Kapleau, Philip. *The Three Pillars of Zen: Teaching, Practice, Enlightenment.* New York: Anchor Books, 1989.
Kostelanetz, Richard. *Conversing With Cage.* New York: Routledge, 2003.
Kosuth, Joseph. 'Art after Philosophy.' 1969. Ed. G. Battcock. *Idea Art: A Critical Anthology.* New York: Dutton, 1973.
—. *Purloined: A Novel.* Cologne: Salon Verlag, 2000.
Kristeva, Julia. *Desire in Language.* 1977. Ed. Leon S. Roudiez. Trans. Thomas Gora, Alice Jardine and Leon S. Roudiez. New York: Columbia UP, 1980.
Kropotkin, Peter. *Mutual Aid: A Factor of Evolution.* 1902. London: Freedom P, 1987.
Lacan, Jacques. *Écrits: A Selection.* Trans. Alan Sheridan. New York: W.W. Norton & Co, 1977.

—. *The Four Fundamental Concepts of Psycho-Analysis*. Trans. Alan Sheridan. New York: W.W. Norton & Co, 1977.

—. *The Seminar of Jacques Lacan Book XVII: The Other Side of Psychoanalysis*. Trans. Russell Grigg. New York: W.W. Norton & Co, 2007.

Lagapa, Jason. 'Something from Nothing: The Disontological Poetics of Leslie Scalapino.' *Contemporary Literature* 47.1 (2006): 30–61.

Lambdin, Thomas O., Trans. *The Gospel of Thomas*. The Gnostic Society Library. 1990. http://www.gnosis.org/naghamm/gthlamb.html. Accessed July 12, 2012.

Larson, Kay. *Where the Heart Beats: John Cage, Zen Buddhism and the Inner Life of Artists*. New York: The Penguin P, 2012.

Laycock, Steven W. *Mind as Mirror and the Mirroring of Mind: Buddhist Reflections on Western Phenomenology*. Albany: SUNY P, 1994.

Lefebvre, Henri. *The Production of Space*. 1974. Trans. Donald Nicholson-Smith. London: Blackwell, 1991.

Leonard, George J. *Into the Light of Things: The Art of the Commonplace from Wordsworth to John Cage*. Chicago: U of Chicago P, 1994.

Lewallen, Constance. *Writings Through John Cage's Music, Poetry and Art*. Eds. David W. Bernstein and Christopher Hatch. Chicago and London: U of Chicago P, 2001, 234–243.

LeWitt, Sol. 'Paragraphs on Conceptual Art.' *Artforum* 5.10 (1967): 8.

Lippard, Lucy. *Six Years: The Dematerialization of the Art Object from 1966–72*. New York: Praeger, 1973.

Longxi, Zhang. 'The Tao and the Logos: Notes on Derrida's Critique of Logocentrism.' *Critical Inquiry* 11 (1985): 385–397.

Luckett, Helen and Lauren A. Wright. 'A Companion to Cage.' *Every Day is a Good Day: The Visual Art of John Cage*. Introduced by Roger Malbert. London: Hayword Publishing, 2010, 55–76.

Mac Low, Jackson. 'Cage's Writings up to the Late 1980s.' *Writings Through John Cage's Music, Poetry, and Art*. Eds. David W. Bernstein and Christopher Hatch. Chicago and London: U of Chicago P, 2001, 210–233.

Marshall, Peter. *Demanding the Impossible: A History of Anarchism*. London: Fontana P, 1993.

McCaffery, Steve. *North of Intention*. Toronto: Nightwood Editions, 1986.

Miles, Barry. Allen *Ginsberg: A Biography*. London: Virgin Books, 2002.

Miller, David. 'The Self and Language in Buddhism (with special reference to Shin Buddhism).' *The Pure Land: Journal of European Shin Buddhism* 3.1 (1981): 34–46.

Moncayo, Raul. 'The Finger Pointing at the Moon: Zen Practice and the Practice of Lacanian Psychoanalysis. *Psychoanalysis and Buddhism: An Unfolding Dialogue*. Ed. Jeremy D. Safran. Boston: Wisdom P, 2003, 331–386.

Mortenson, Eric. 'Keeping Vision Alive: The Buddhist Stillpoint in the Work of Jack Kerouac and Allen Ginsberg.' *The Emergence of Buddhist American Literature*. Eds. John Whalen-Bridge and Gary Storhoff. Albany: SUNY P, 2009, 123–138.
Newman, Saul. *From Bakunin to Lacan: Anti-Authoritarianism and the Dislocation of Power.* Lanham: Lexington Books, 2001.
Nicholls, David. *John Cage*. Urbana and Chicago: U of Illinois P, 2007.
Olson, Charles. *Collected Prose*. Eds. Donald Allen and Benjamin Friedlander. Los Angles: U of California P, 1997.
—. *The Maximus Poems*. 1960; 1968; 1975. Berkeley: U of California P, 1983.
Patterson, David W. 'The Picture That is Not in the Colors: Cage, Coomaraswamy, and the Impact of India.' *John Cage: Music, Philosophy, and Intention, 1933–1950*. Ed. David W. Patterson. London: Routledge, 2002, 177–215.
Perloff, Marjorie. *The Poetics of Indeterminacy: Rimbaud to Cage*. Princeton: Princeton UP, 1981.
—. *Radical Artifice: Writing Poetry in the Age of Media*. Chicago: University of Chicago Press, 1991.
Pritchett, James. *The Music of John Cage*. Cambridge: Cambridge UP, 1993.
Reps, Paul. *Zen Flesh, Zen Bones: A Collection of Zen and Pre-Zen Writings*. New York: Doubleday and Co., 1957.
Retallack, Joan. 'Poethics of a Complex Realism' *John Cage: Composed in America*. Eds. Marjorie Perloff and Charles Junkerman. Chicago: U of Chicago P, 1994, 242–273.
Revill, David. *The Roaring Silence: John Cage: A Life*. London: Bloomsbury, 1992.
Roberts, Jennifer L. *Robert Smithson and History*. New Haven and London: Yale University Press, 2004.
Ross, Andrew. 'Taking the Tennis Court Oath.' *The Tribes of John: Ashbery and Contemporary Poetry*. Ed. Susan M. Schultz. Tuscaloosa: U of Alabama P, 1995, 193–210.
Ross, Stephen. 'A Very Brief Introduction to Lacan.' http://web.uvic.ca/~saross/lacan.html. Accessed October 18, 2010.
Sangharakshita. *Crossing the Stream: Reflections on the Buddhist Spiritual Path*. Birmingham: Windhorse, 1987.
—. *The Essence of Zen*. Birmingham: Windhorse, 1973.
—. *What is the Dharma? The Essential Teachings of the Buddha*. Birmingham: Windhorse Publications, 1998.
Scalapino, Leslie. *How Phenomena Appear to Unfold*. Elmwood: Potes & Poets P, 1989.
—. 'Language as Transient Act, The Poetry of Philip Whalen.' *Collected Poems of Philip Whalen*. Ed. Michael Rothenberg. Lebanon, NH: Wesleyan UP, 2007.

—. *New Time*. Hanover: Wesleyan UP, 1999.
—. *that they were at the beach – aelotropic series*. San Francisco: North Point P, 1985.
Schafer, R. Murray. *The Soundscape: Our Sonic Environment and the Tuning of the World*. Rochester, Vermont: Destiny Books, 1994.
Sekida, Katsuki. *Two Zen Classics: Mumonkan and Hekiganroku*. Trans. Katsuki Sekida. New York: Weatherhill, 1977.
Seng-t'san. 'Verses on the Faith of Mind' (ebook). Trans. D.T. Suzuki. Vipassati Philosophical Practice. http://www.vipassati.ch/english/books/Verses-on-the-Faith-in-Mind-Suzuki_ebook.html. Accessed May 19, 2011.
Shute, Clarence. 'The Comparative Phenomenology of Japanese Painting and Zen Buddhism.' *Philosophy East and West* 18 (1968): 285–298.
Silverman, Kenneth. *Begin Again: A Biography of John Cage*. New York: Alfred A. Knopf, 2010.
Simms, Bryan R. *Music of the Twentieth Century: Style and Structure*. London: Collier Macmillan, 1986.
Skinner, Jonathan. 'Statement on 'New Nature Writing.' *Ecopoetics* no. 4/5 (2005): 127–129.
—. 'Thoughts on Things: Poetics of the Third Landscape.' *The Eco Language Reader*. Ed. Brenda Iijima. New York: Portable Press at Yo-Yo Labs/Nightboat Books, 2010.
Smithson, Robert. *Robert Smithson: The Collected Writings*. Ed. Jack Flam. Berkeley: University of California Press, 1996.
Snelling, John. *The Buddhist Handbook: A Complete Guide to Buddhist Teaching and Practice*. London: Rider, 1987.
Snyder, Gary. 'Buddhist Anarchism.' 1961. *Bureau of Public Secrets*. http://www.bopsecrets.org/CF/garysnyder.htm. Accessed February 7, 2012.
—. 'By Frazier Creek Falls.' *The Gary Snyder Reader: Prose, Poetry and Translations*. New York: Counterpoint P, 1999, 477.
Spahr, Juliana, Mark Wallace, Kristen Prevallet and Pam Rehm, Eds. *A Poetics of Criticism*. Buffalo: Leave Books, 1994.
Steinberg, Michael. 'Tradition and Responsibility.' *Perspectives of New Music* 1 (1964): 154–159.
Suzuki, Daisetz Teitaro. *An Introduction to Zen Buddhism*. Foreword by C.G. Jung. NY: Grove Press, 1948.
—. *An Introduction to Zen Buddhism*. Ed. Christmas Humphreys. London: Rider & Co., 1949.
—. *Essays in Zen Buddhism*. First Series. London: Rider and Co, 1949.
—. *The Essentials of Zen Buddhism: An Anthology of the Writings of Daisetz T. Suzuki*. Ed. Bernard Philips. London: Rider & Co., 1963.

—. *The Lankavātāra Sutra: A Mahāyāna Text.* 1932. Buddhist Tradition Series, Vol. 40. Delhi: Motilal Banarsidass Publishers, 2009.
—. *Living by Zen.* Ed. Christmas Humphreys. London: Rider & Co., 1950.
—. *Manual of Zen Buddhism.* New York: Grove, 1960.
—. *Mysticism Christian and Buddhist.* New York; Harper & Brothers, 1957.
—. *The Zen Doctrine of No Mind.* Ed. Christmas Humphreys. London: Rider and Co, 1949.
Tan, Kathy Ann. *The Non-conformist's Poem: Radical 'Poetics of Autobiography' in the Works of Lyn Hejinian, Susan Howe and Leslie Scalapino.* Trier: Wissenschaflicher Verlag Trier, 2008.
Tan, Margaret Leng. '*4'33"*: A Zen Perspective.' John Cage 100 Symposium. Lublin, Poland. May 17, 2012.
Tarlo, Harriet. 'Recycles: the Eco-Ethical Poetics of Found Text in Contemporary Poetry.' *Journal of Ecocriticism* 1.2 (2009): 114–130.
Thoreau, Henry David. *A Week on the Concord and Merrimack Rivers.* 1849. Eds. Carl F. Hovde, William L. Howarth and Elizabeth Hall Witherell. Witherell: Princeton UP, 1980.
—. *The Journal of Henry David Thoreau.* 1858. Ed. Walter Harding. New York: Dover, 1962.
Thurman, Robert A. F., trans. *The Holy Teaching of Vimalakīrti: A Mahāyāna Scripture.* London: Pennsylvania State UP, 1976.
Trigilio, Tony. *Allen Ginsberg's Buddhist Poetics.* Carbondale: Southern Illinois UP, 2007.
Tu Shun. 'Cessation and Contemplation in the Five Teachings of the Hua-yen.' *Entry into the Inconceivable: An Introduction to Hua-yen Buddhism.* Ed. Thomas Cleary. Honolulu: U of Hawaii P, 1983, 43–68.
Watts, Alan W. *Beat Zen Square Zen and Zen.* San Francisco: City Lights Books, 1959.
—. *The Way of Zen.* London: Thames & Hudson, 1957.
Whalen, Philip. *Collected Poems of Philip Whalen.* Ed. Michael Rothenberg. Lebanon, NH: Wesleyan UP, 2007.
—. 'Philip Whalen: Zen Interview.' Interview with Andrew Schelling and Anne Waldman. *Disembodied Poetics.* Eds. Anne Waldman and Andrew Schelling. Albuquerque: University of New Mexico P, 1994, 224–237.
Williams, Paul, with Anthony Tribe. *Buddhist Thought: A Complete Introduction to the Indian Tradition.* London: Routledge, 2000.
—. *Mahāyāna Buddhism: The Doctrinal Foundations.* London: Routledge, 1989.
Yamada, Kōun Roshi. *The Gateless Gate: The Classic Book of Zen Kōans.* Somerville MA: Wisdom Publications, 2004.

Yamada, Mumon. 'Taken from Lectures on the Zazen-Gi.' *How to Practice Zazen.* Trans. Eshin Nishimura. Kyoto: Institute for Zen Studies, no date, 1–28.

Žižek, Slavoj. *Looking Awry: An Introduction to Jacques Lacan through Popular Culture.* Cambridge, MA: MIT P, 1991.

—. *On Belief.* London: Routledge, 2001.

—. *The Sublime Object of Ideology.* London: Verso, 1989.

—. *Tarrying with the Negative.* Durham: Duke UP, 1993.

Index

Acconci, Vito 71
Adam, Michael 48
Anarchism 103, 141–2, 147–9, 152–61
Anātman 34, 45, 96, 148
Ashbery, John 72–3
Avatamsaka Sutra 55–6

Bachelard, Gaston 5, 35–7
Bal, Mieke 3, 27–8
Basho, Matsuo 52
Bataille, Georges 134–5
Batchelor, Martine 55–6
Batchelor, Stephen 55
Berrigan, Ted 72–3
Berry, Wendell 66
Black Mountain College 19, 167n. 1
Blofeld, John 12
Bloom, Ina 132–3
Bodhidharma 80, 136, 168n. 11
Brown, Norman O. 39, 164
Bryson, J. Scott 2
Buddha 10–14, 24, 38, 45, 55–8, 68, 102, 106, 167n. 3, 169n. 13

Cage, John, Works by:
 4'33" 1
 A Year From Monday: New Lectures and Writings 137
 Anarchy 152, 154–6, 160
 "Composition as Process" 8, 26, 31–2, 85, 103–4
 "Diary: How to Improve the World (You Will Only Make Matters Worse) 1965" 138–9
 Empty Words: Writing '73–'78 5, 26–9, 59–60, 77–80, 95, 127, 154
 "Experimental Music" 11
 For the Birds: In Conversation with Daniel Charles 12, 43, 57, 76, 82, 90, 147, 152, 168n. 12
 "Indeterminacy: New Aspects of Form in Instrumental and Electronic Music" 18, 25
 "Lecture on Nothing" 7–8, 34–8, 76, 84–5
 "Lecture on the Weather" 66
 M: Writings '67–'72 39–40, 66–7, 164–5
 "36 Mesostics Re and not RE Marcel Duchamp" 40–1
 Mureau 5, 66–8, 127
 "On Robert Rauschenberg, Artist and his Work" 54–7
 "Overpopulation and Art" 102–3
 Silence 3, 5, 8–10, 18–19, 23–5, 31, 37, 44, 47–8, 51, 54–7, 60, 69–70, 76, 82, 100–16, 138, 154, 166

"Water Walk" 1
"Where Are We Going? And What Are We Doing?" 110, 112
Chandrakanthan, A. J. V. 11
Charles, Daniel 12, 75, 89, 151
Christensen, Paul 91, 94
Chuang-tse 141–2
Clark, Tom 93–4
Cleary, Thomas 50
Clough, Bradley F. 159
Coomaraswamy, Ananda 53–4, 69–70
Culver, Andrew 4
Curtin, Deane 105–6

Deleuze, Gilles and Felix Guattari 38
Dōgen 48, 58–9, 105–6, 109
Dworkin, Craig 72, 171n. 2

Eckhart, Meister 25, 99–101
Evans, Dylan 117, 125

Falk, Jane 91, 96–8
Fink, Bruce 119–20
Fitterman, Robert 73, 78
Freud, Sigmund 44, 170n. 19
Frost, Elizabeth A. 107
Fuller, Buckminster 172n. 7

Gallop, Jane 117
Gifford, Terry 61
Ginsberg, Allen 78, 80, 86–90, 96
Glass, N. Robert 38
Goldman, Emma 154
Goldsmith, Kenneth 70, 84
Gospel of Thomas, The 103

Hanh, Thich Nhat 157–60, 167n. 8
Harris, Ian 58

Heart of Perfect Wisdom Sutra 66
Hekiganroku 31–2
Hilson, Jeff 59–61
Holquist, Michael 118
Hseih Ho 53
Huang-Po Doctrine of Universal Mind, The 12–15, 68
Hua-Yen School 55–6, 68
Humphreys, Christmas 136

I Ching 4–6, 67, 95, 168n. 6
indeterminacy 1, 5, 20, 25–30, 51, 59, 102, 123, 128, 160
Indra's Net 55–6

Jagodzinski, Jan 146
Jakobson, Roman 118
Joyce, James 74
Jung, C. G. 115, 171n. 1

Kahn, Douglas 132
Kapleau, Philip 82, 136, 148
Karuna 70
Kegon Buddhism see Hua-Yen School
Kenshō 22, 97, 138
Kōans 10, 17–23, 31, 59, 97, 128
Kostelanetz, Richard 80
Kosuth, Joseph 71
Kōun Yamada Roshi 19–20, 97, 167n. 3
Kristeva, Julia 143
Kropotkin, Peter 152–4
Kyōgen 97

Lacan, Jacques 5, 20–1, 116–29, 144–6
Lagapa, Jason 108
Larson, Kay 2
Laycock, Steven W. 38
Lefebvre, Henri 131
Leonard, George G. 140–1

Lewallen, Constance 4
LeWitt, Sol 74–5
Lippard, Lucy 75
Longxi, Zhang 143
Luckett, Helen 31

McCaffery, Steve 135
Mahākāśyapa 13–14
Mac Low, Jackson 7, 112–13, 115
McLuhan, Marshall 155
Mao-tse-Tung 154
Marshall, Peter 142, 149
Mesostics 39–43, 102, 152–3
Miles, Barry 87
Miller, David 17, 38
Moncayo, Raul 177
Mortenson, Eric 115
Mumonkan 10, 19

Nāgārjuna 42–3
Naropa Institute 77–80
Newman, Saul 144, 147–8
Nicholls, David 4
nothing 5, 29, 44, 59, 80, 99, 100, 119, 123–5, 127, 131–3, 135, 144–5, 147, 151 *passim*

Olson, Charles 7–9, 72–3, 87, 167n. 1

Patris, Aimé 134
Patterson, David W. 53
Perloff, Marjorie 18–19, 22, 41–2
Place, Vanessa 73
Pound, Ezra 87
Prajña 17
Pseudo-Dionysius 101

Ramakrishna, Sri 25, 171n. 23
Rauschenberg, Robert 54–7
Reps, Paul 11

Retallack, Joan 156, 166
Ross, Andrew 72

Sangharakshita 12, 24, 46, 167n. 4
Satori 22, 51, 87
Scalapino, Leslie 106–10
Schafer, R. Murray 60
Schelling, Andrew 6
Sekida, Katsuki 31
Seng-t'san 95
Shute, Clarence 97
Silverman, Kenneth 2, 80
Simms, Bryan R. 25–6
Skinner, Jonathan 2, 64–5
Smithson, Robert 64–5, 68, 169n. 18
Snelling, John 47, 56, 62
Snyder, Gary 60–3, 150–1
Steinberg, Michael 132
Suiwō 50
Śūnyatā 16, 20, 29, 34, 43, 47, 71, 86, 99, 105, 115, 167n. 4
Suzuki, Daisetz Teitaro 13, 15, 22–4, 40, 50–3, 56, 58, 68–9, 99, 103, 115, 167n. 2, 168n. 10, 169n. 13, 171n. 22, 172n. 3

Tan, Kathy Ann 107
Tan, Margaret Leng 1
Taoism 4, 141–3, 153–4
Tarlo, Harriet 169n. 17
Thoreau, Henry David 66–7, 74, 78, 95, 128, 154
Thurman, Robert 11, 29, 65, 167n. 4
Trigilio, Tony 88
Trungpa, Chögyam Rinpoche 78, 86–8
Tu Shun 55–7
Tudor, David 19–22, 167n. 1, 172n. 4

Unmon 31

Vimalakriī Nirdeśa 11

Waldman, Anne 78
Watts, Alan W. 15, 50–2, 70, 168n. 12
Wei Yuan 143

Whalen, Philip 6, 90–8, 109
Williams, Paul 17, 49, 77

Yamada, Mumon 49
Yogācarā 17

Žižek, Slavoj 119, 122, 126–30, 136–7, 162

www.ingramcontent.com/pod-product-compliance
Lightning Source LLC
Chambersburg PA
CBHW040904250426
43673CB00064B/1953